THE NEW YORK DOLLS

TOO MUCH TOO SOON

THE NEW YORK DOLLS

TOO MUCH TOO SOON

NINA ANTONIA

OMNIBUS PRESS

LONDON / NEW YORK / PARIS / SYDNEY / COPENHAGEN / BERLIN / MADRID / TOKYO

Edited by Chris Charlesworth
Cover designed by Philip Gambrill
Picture research by Nikki Russell

ISBN: 0.7119.9603.2
Order No: OP49181

Exclusive Distributors:
Book Sales Limited,
8/9 Frith Street,
London W1V 5TZ, UK.

Music Sales Corporation,
257 Park Avenue South,
New York, NY 10010, USA.

Macmillan Distribution Services,
53 Park West Drive,
Derrimut, Vic 3030,
Australia.

To the Music Trade only:
Music Sales Limited,
8/9 Frith Street,
London W1V 5TZ, UK.

Photo credits:
Every effort has been made to trace the copyright holders of the photo-
graphs in this book but one or two were unreachable. We would be grateful
if the photographers concerned would contact us.

Cover photo: Bob Gruen.

Typeset by Galleon Typesetting, Ipswich.
Printed in Great Britain.

A catalogue record for this book is available from the British Library.

Visit Omnibus Press at http://www.omnibuspress.com

Contents

Acknowledgements and Sentiments

My gratitude goes out to everybody who agreed to be interviewed. I would especially like to thank Peter Jordan and Sylvain Sylvain.

I would also like to acknowledge the contributions of the following: Mariann Bracken & family, Chris Charlesworth, Randy Chase at Fishhead Records, Tom Crossley, Rob Dimery, Eve & Neil, George Gimarc, Clinton Heylin, Olga Larrett, Freddie Lynxx (for his discography), Pedro Mercedes, John Perry, Phyllis Stein. And of course, my dear Severina.

This book is dedicated to the memories of Billy Murcia, Johnny Thunders and Jerry Nolan, for whom it is too little, too late.

Introduction

"If this film's an exit sign, then my deity's a mirage, like the image of heaven must be to men kneeling down at an altar. It's just some lost artist's or artists' wild stab in the dark at how life in the clouds would seem. It's scratchy, underlit. But it's the only idea in this theater that hasn't burned out yet . . ."

(From *Wrong* by Dennis Cooper)

The New York Dolls put the Chaos Theory into rock'n'roll. Like the butterfly that rippled against an oncoming storm, causing a momentary rift in the flow of the universe that subsequently built up into a fearsome hurricane, few remember or even refer to the original creature of chaos, they just recall the consequences.

The New York Dolls were the Bowery butterflies that irrevocably altered the course of rock'n'roll. Their actual moment, 1971–1975, was brief but their influence, whether acknowledged or not, spans two decades. At various times during their fabulous reign heinous attempts were made to suppress their career by a conservative core within the music business. The Dolls appeared to prevail but they weren't dancing, they were falling.

One boy's 'good time' is another's booze-fuelled pill-popping endless party. The New York Dolls were a high time, high-wire act without a safety net. Their music reflected perfectly both the New York of the early Seventies and their own high intensity dramas: tom-toms beat over Manhattan, guitars wailed like cop car sirens, the vocals were guttural street corner captions, emphasised by sloppy kisses and wolf-whistles, silenced by a gun shot. Dirty angels with painted faces, the Dolls opened the box usually reserved for Pandora and unleashed the infant furies that would grow to become Punk. As if this legacy wasn't enough for one band, they also trashed sexual boundaries, savaged glitter and set new standards for rock'n'roll excess.

The Dolls' nonchalant acts of artistic vandalism and liberation have long outlived them but their monument, if there was one, would surely stand on unhallowed ground, for they came in the end to represent all that is considered debauched in rock culture. In the twenty or so years since their demise, the Dolls have become a perpetual reference point as *the* archetypal, hedonistic rock'n'roll band. For their sins, The New York Dolls have been constantly ostracised by the guardians of the mainstream but are nevertheless revered by a legion of devotees and recognised by the media cognoscenti. Over the years a series of bands have covered Dolls' tracks. Fragments of details rise to the surface in occasional documentaries. A car rips around a corner to a blast of the Dolls in a recent television commercial, yet the band isn't credited for it. The New York Dolls have pervaded contemporary culture but they do so in a glamorous semi-obscurity which is pretty much how it was when they were still together.

1
Baby Dolls

The New York Dolls may have looked like they just stepped right out of Manhattan Babylon as fully formed teenage transvestite hookers with street manners but they were not children of the inner city. They came from refugee, migrant and exiled stock, and they came of age in New York's outer boroughs where their families had settled in the Fifties.

Of the five principal boys, Sylvain Sylvain, christened Ronald Mizrahi, travelled the furthest, from Cairo to New York via Paris. Following the Suez Canal crisis in 1956, Sylvain's father lost his job as a banker in Cairo and, as Egyptian Jews, the family were forced into exile and obliged to relinquish their home and most of their possessions. Regardless of the political traumas, little Sylvain was enriched by a childhood spent in Cairo. Sylvain: "There's an Arab instrument called the oud, it looks like a guitar but it's got a round back. The Arabs make them by hand and my father bought me a child-size one. I'll never forget the beat of Arabic music, it's got an incredible rhythm."

Sylvain, his elder brother and parents boarded a Greek merchant ship bound for France, then journeyed to Paris where they lived in a hotel room in the artists' quarter of Montmartre. With the help of a Jewish resettlement scheme, the Mizrahi family applied to go to the United States, crossing the Atlantic in 1961. Sylvain: "I remember when we cruised into the harbour, it was rainy and cloudy. Me and my brother were on the deck and we saw the Statue of Liberty. To me the whole image of the United States was tall buildings, like New York. I was really taken in by the commercials of the time. I

9

thought that every girl would look like Marilyn Monroe and that for breakfast you'd have Bazooka bubblegum and then Coca-Cola for dinner!"

Sylvain and his family were housed in Buffalo, which they were shocked to find was closer to Niagara Falls than New York city. They hastily relocated to Brooklyn before settling down in the borough of Queens, a largely family orientated district that boasts Shea Stadium as one of its most famous landmarks. The lawns of Queens are mowed with efficient regularity and the cars on its streets are polished to perfection. It's enough to turn any kid with a rebel streak towards rock'n'roll.

Sylvain was dispatched to Van Wyck junior high in Jamaica, a Queens neighbourhood, where his non-existent grasp of English made him an easy target. Sylvain: "The first words I ever learned in English was 'Fuck you'. The other kids would come up to me and say 'You speak English?' and I would say 'No'. They would go 'Fuck you'. He quickly learned to adopt a wily self-protective attitude which was put to the test when an older boy, Alphonso Murcia, challenged Syl to a fight with his younger brother, Billy. When he issued the playground challenge Alphonso didn't realise that Billy and Syl were already acquainted, and the ensuing scrap was largely a put on. Sylvain: "We weren't friends but we weren't enemies either. Billy was like 'C'mon, let's go.' He had a lot of surly moves. We scuffled a little, kicked up some dust. It was more like a cartoon than a fight. Then we said, 'Why the fuck are we fighting?'. We became the best of friends."

Their two halves of broken English made a whole and they rapidly became inseparable. From a distance, the two boys resembled a romantic notion of gypsy twins with their dark features and wild corkscrew hair. Up close however, Syl looked like an exotic relative of Marc Bolan while Billy was slightly more muscular, with a defined, angular face and large plaintive eyes that more often than not were obscured by a curtain of ringlets.

Billy and his family's flight from their home in Bogota, the crime-ridden capital of Colombia, had been no less dramatic than Sylvain's flight from Cairo. Papa Murcia was an inventive businessman with a penchant for racing cars and speed boats. Unfortunately, he ran into trouble with hostile bandidos after opening an ice-skating rink with the wrong business partner. Putting his family's safety before everything else, Mr Murcia gathered up his three offspring, Alphonso, Billy and Heidi, and their mother, Mercedes, packed as much as they could carry and hightailed it to America. They took up residence in a large old house in Jamaica not far from where Sylvain's family had settled and made ends meet by renting out the spare rooms to other immigrants. Sylvain was practically adopted by the Murcia clan and even moved his bed into the spacious wood panelled basement where he and Billy established a den.

The two boys left Van Wyck for New Town High, also in Queens. In the corridors or out in the playground, they kept catching glimpses of a striking looking Italian-American kid with daringly long black hair. Even though they didn't hang out with Johnny Genzale, they'd heard that he was a mean baseball player and figured that he must be pretty cool. Johnny was such a quiet, shy boy, his demeanour almost masked his emotional instability. It was as though he had a slow burning fuse that would ignite when something bothered him and more often than not that was the school's rules and regulations. Johnny: "I hated school. I always did terrible, couldn't wait to leave." Although he'd been spared the trauma of the geographical displacement suffered by his grandparents when they left their native Naples and Sicily in favour of a new life in America, he was still insecure. His father, Emil, an attractive lady-killer who preferred slow dancing in smoky clubs to pram pushing in the park, walked out on his mother when Johnny was just a baby. With no financial assistance, Josephine Genzale had to work two jobs to support Johnny, who was left in the care of his elder sister Mariann.

By the time Johnny reached his early teens, the past was just a dull ache, that is until he became a prominent figure in the

11

neighbourhood Little League baseball team. Johnny: "I used to play baseball from eight in the morning till eight the next night and loved it." His passion almost paid off when he was scouted by the Philadelphia Phillies. However, in those days it was a requirement of the Little League that all fathers, without exception, should also be involved in team activities and Johnny lost his place. He would later cover up the truth by telling journalists he quit baseball when the coach demanded that he cut his hair.

What was baseball's loss became rock'n'roll's gain. Johnny threw down the bat, picked up a bass guitar and recruited some high school pals for a band. When Mariann got a job with a small catering firm, she started to get her little brother bookings for barmitzvahs, birthdays and weddings. Amidst the crepe paper and confetti, Johnny and The Jaywalkers débuted wearing matching non-crease nylon suits, belting out standards in the back of a church hall. They would later change their name to Reign.

Of the original nucleus that made up The New York Dolls, there was one other founder member, Arthur Harold Kane. A tall blond of Irish descent who came from the Bronx, Kane was a complete physical contradiction to the Queens contingent of petite brunettes. There is something faraway about Arthur. He has the presence of an apparition with the tiniest voice you've ever heard, like a talking toy with the wrong batteries. Arthur Kane was a loner and a straight A student until circumstances flipped his dials. He had not yet acquired George Fedorcik as a best friend but they shared an English class. George: "I didn't like him at first, he was a very quiet and a very smart student and he was really serious about school until his mother died, then he seemed to totally lose it and got involved in drugs and drinking."

After his mother's death, Arthur dived head first into rock'n'roll and started playing rhythm guitar in a band with George. He also burned any of the bridges that could possibly have led him back to a straighter, safer life. George: "I considered Arthur to be my brother. He was just the coolest guy that I knew, he was way ahead of his time as far as fashion went. He was the first person I knew who wore bellbottoms. The other kids in high school used to really break his balls about the way he looked."

For nearly all kids, the mid-teens are the crucial turning point when the world suddenly expands beyond the immediate vicinity. The boys in the Dolls were no exception, but the fact that they all looked to New York City as the centre of adventure meant they got street sophisticated faster than most.

Arthur graduated to the arts based Pratt College to study hotel management, perhaps he'd had Bates Motel in mind when he signed up for the course. He dropped out in early 1970 and embarked upon a head-spinning spree with George, fired up on glue, acid and alcohol. George: "We both got really heavily into acid but I can't believe that at 18 we were still doing glue. We used to get big quarts of rubber cement glue and sniff it. It really messes you up. Arthur was always very quiet, he really never had much to say on anything. He would just go along with things or do stupid stuff."

Their biggest turn-ons were near miss auto incidents and psychedelic surfing. George: "One time in the middle of winter, we drove to Times Square with the top down on the car, and we got into an accident with a cab. The cab driver wanted to kick my ass. As he was trying to pull me out of the car, Arthur was just sitting there going 'Everything's cool, everything's cool'. Arthur was a terrible driver . . . when he got his licence he had five accidents in one week and wrecked his father's Tempest. We used to go surfing all the time . . . we never were any good at it but it was cool on acid and pot. I remember once we were on the parkway and the surfboard went flying off the top of the car and caused a big crash, everybody was swerving to a halt. I wouldn't get out of the car and I said 'Arthur, go out and get the board'. Then we got a Volkswagen van together."

The highlight of being a cool kid in the city was the Sunday afternoon promenade that took place around the fountain in Central Park. Outwardly a casual gathering, it was an opportunity for the teens to preen. Although he didn't say too much, hidden by his long teased hair that resembled raven's wings in a storm, Johnny Genzale and his girlfriend Janis Cafasso talked volumes when it came to style. Arthur: "We'd all get dressed up to the teeth and go to Central Park on a Sunday. There was nothing else to do. It was after the Sixties when there had been love-ins and be-ins and everyone was on LSD, taking their clothes off and going crazy in the same place in Central Park, but it had become a little more sedate. People were there to look at each other and I saw Johnny around that time with his girlfriend, Janis, who dressed up like a Raggedy Ann doll, she had this long red curly hair and red rouge on her cheeks. Johnny had all that hair and the first time I noticed him he was wearing a green velvet suit. Then I saw him a couple more times in these other outfits that you just couldn't find, 'cos I tried, I went to thrift shops and rooted everything out. Then I discovered that Johnny was buying his clothes in women's shops, downtown on Orchard Street and his mom or sister would tailor them for him, so he was wearing these customised suits all the time. Very impressive."

After quitting school in a deluge of bad behaviour reports, Johnny pleaded with his mother to send him to a private, liberal establishment called Quintanos. Located in the back of Carnegie Hall and just two blocks away from Central Park, the aim of Quintanos was to groom students for careers in the performing arts. However, even classes held in the park with a steady supply of reefer weren't enough to keep Johnny G interested. He left home and Quintanos at sixteen and began to do the rounds of the rock'n'roll circuit. There was the Action House, a rock club out on Long Island, Nobody's bar on Bleecker street, a favourite groupie haunt populated by British bands passing through town, and the Fillmore East for live rock shows. Arthur and best buddy George were on nodding terms with Johnny. George: "We used to see Johnny at the Fillmore every time there'd be a British band playing. We were totally into the English scene – The Stones, The Yardbirds. We never really spoke to Johnny but we'd always say 'Hi' because of the way he looked. We thought he was the coolest thing in the world."

Someone else who thought Johnny looked pretty good was Janis Cafasso. Along with her cousin, Gail Higgins Smith, Janis would drive into the city from Long Island every weekend to catch the bands at the Fillmore. Johnny and Janis embarked on a big romance. After checking out San Francisco together, the three of them found an apartment between 9th and 10th street in the East Village. Janis, who was heavily into fashion and would find a future in design, further exaggerated Johnny's appearance, introducing a feminine element to his look. In between all the dress-up sessions, there were gigs to go to. Gail Higgins Smith: "Me, Johnny and Janis were big rock'n'roll fans. We went anywhere to see a rock'n'roll band and to meet rock'n'roll people. Somehow, because we were brazen, we'd always end up meeting them. When we went to the Newport Jazz festival we ended up sitting in a hotel room with Rod Stewart drinking beer. We met Janis Joplin, and the MC5 who were Johnny's heroes. He was so excited when he met Keith Richards. He would talk about him all the time. We met him at a bar on 5th Avenue and 13th Street. People like Jagger, Richards and Lennon used to go there and one night Keith Richards was there. We sat around this table, having drinks and meeting Keith. Johnny used to say, 'I want to be a pop star, I want to be like Keith Richards'. He even kept Keith's cigarette packet."

Despite the widespread belief that The New York Dolls were all street urchins with little or no sense of what lay beyond Manhattan – "Wha'choo mean? Dere's more to Englan' dan da Stones" – all the founding Dolls visited Europe at a time when the dollar was particularly strong. Johnny: "A friend of mine in New York was working for a magazine so I got to borrow their press pass and when me and a girlfriend came to England we just kinda went around checkin' out all these bands for free, I saw mustabeen fifty or sixty bands. I saw Tyrannosaurus Rex, stuff like that. It wasn't long after I went home that I got into music myself."

Arthur and George set off for Amsterdam where they tried to get a band together but failed to find a vocalist who could sing in English. In spite of their long, straggly hair, there was no way Arthur and George would have classed each other as hippies. They modelled themselves on the English rock star look, and bought their clothes in Jumping Jack Flash and Granny Takes a Trip in New York. They got by in Holland selling 'keef', a particularly potent strain of hashish. In Pamela Des Barre's autobiography *I'm With The Band*, the celebrated groupie and former member of Frank Zappa's GTO's chronicles her brief spell in Amsterdam, where she worked up the fare to England by selling keef for some hippies. Arthur and George had been happy to help Miss Pamela and her friend, Renee, but would've cringed had they known that one day she would refer to them as 'hippies' in her memoirs. Pamela Des Barres: "The hippies sold keef, a crumbly, potent ochre-coloured substance, stronger than hash. I was flat out of dough, so Renee and I went to a sleazy club called the Milweg (Milkyway) and sold a ton of it to the locals. For a few days we made the rounds of the hostels, selling it to the travelling students, and one afternoon I decided to try a dab of the merchandise. I landed face down on another planet."

George returned home after their money and keef supply dried up. Not long after his departure, Arthur was arrested and deported. Kane had been mooching around a flea market when he spied a second-hand motorbike for sale. As he rode the motorbike out of the market he was stopped by the police who discovered that the bike the American had just purchased was stolen property. On further investigation they discovered that Arthur's visa had expired and that he was in possession of a small amount of hashish. Arthur Kane was promptly escorted to the airport.

Back in New York, Arthur and George rented an apartment on 10th Street and First Avenue. Arthur started working for the telephone company while George took a job with the post office. Not content with regular paychecks that suit regular guys, they got serious about the band thing they were always talking about. As a mark of his rock star intentions, George Fedorcik began calling himself Rick Rivets.

The only boys who had thus far got any real mileage out of their rock'n'roll dreams were Billy and Syl and they hadn't got much further than a block or two, with their first group The Pox. After splitting school, Billy took up playing drums and was tutored by Sylvain who taught him to swing sticks along to The Surfari's hectic instrumental 'Wipeout'. For Murcia, once described as 'a cool drink of water with a hot head', playing drums was like throwing a tantrum, a natural outlet. The Pox broke out when Syl and Billy hooked up with Mike Turby, a local hero who had gained neighbourhood notoriety with The Orphans – Queens answer to The Rolling Stones. Turby, an accomplished guitarist, put Billy and Syl through their musical paces, giving instruction where before there had been only enthusiasm.

In 1968 The Pox signed a contract and cut a demo for would-be record tycoon Harry Lookofsky, father of keyboard player Mike Brown from The Left Banke. Lookofsky had been responsible for the baroque production on 'Walk Away Renee' which gave the Left Banke a top ten US hit in 1966. Sylvain: "The Pox was a three piece, we were a little like the early Who with the influence of the music that was coming out of Detroit back then, like Iggy and The Stooges. We used to play 'No Fun'. We did a gig at the Hotel Diplomat on 43rd Street. It had a grand ballroom that they used to rent out to hippies once a week and we supported this band called The Group Image. They had a girl singer called Barbara who eventually married Arthur Kane. We opened up for them, Michael Turby was playing bass, Billy was on drums and I turned my amp right up and started riffing. The audience went nuts, then we started our repertoire with this song 'Epitaph' and Group Image pulled the plug on us. Billy kept on playing and the kids kept on cheering. That was our introduction to the cut-throat business of rock'n'roll!"

When The Pox failed to reach epidemic proportions, Mike Turby left for San Francisco while Syl and Billy did time in Quintanos school. Taking their cues from the two things they loved best, rock'n'roll and cool clothes, the dandy duo got busy with their own fashion outlet, Truth & Soul. Sylvain got his retail experience working at the happening men's boutique The Different Drummer on Lexington Avenue and 63rd Street. Across the road from the store was a fixed sign on the front of an old brownstone building which read The New York Doll's Hospital. A million of the city's brokenhearted children had tramped up the scuffed stairs carrying their damaged dolls into this toy ER, and as he gazed at the sign Sylvain wondered if Billy would think it was as great a name for a band as he did.

One afternoon Syl watched his future walk right past The Doll's Hospital like a trailer for a forthcoming movie. Sylvain: "I saw Janis and Johnny go by, holding hands. Now, this was the time when *Gimme Shelter* was playing. Me and Billy were in love with that movie and Johnny is in it. He's fooling around with his hair, sitting on one of his friend's shoulders. It's in the sequence when the lights get turned on the audience and Mick Jagger say's something like 'New York, let's look at you, now.' We used to see it every other day and we'd go 'Hey man, there's that fucking guy we used to go to school with!' "

Sylvain quit The Different Drummer to concentrate fully on Truth & Soul. Inspired by the brightly coloured and patterned woollens that are traditionally worn in Colombia, Billy and Sylvain set about making psychedelic sweaters on a hand loom. Orders started coming in from the ultra-hip Betsey Johnson, and the duo also made psychedelic bikini tops for Paraphernalia. As the orders piled up, Mercedes Murcia brought over a master loomer from Colombia to expand the operation. Following a complimentary write-up in the prestigious *Women's Wear Daily*, Truth & Soul sold their designs for mass production to the Nausbaum knitting mills in Brooklyn. Splitting the ample proceeds between them, Billy went to Amsterdam and Syl to England.

For close on a year, Billy and Alphonso Murcia bummed around Holland. When all their money had gone up in smoke in Amsterdam's hash cafes, Billy took to busking with his bongos. Sylvain managed to track down his pal and found him hunched up, cross-legged on the street, fighting with his older brother. Syl promptly whisked him off to England. He'd had a ball in London and the only serious money he'd spent had gone on three Marshall amps, which were shipped back to the Murcia's basement. Sylvain had shopped till he dropped, and hung out on The King's Road until he'd absorbed every retail detail of the pop couture promenade. He'd struck up an acquaintance with Trevor Miles, who specialised in groovy vintage threads and had a shop on 430 King's Road called Paradise Garage. The following year Miles would turn over the premises to Malcolm McLaren and Vivienne Westwood.

By the close of 1970, Syl and Billy were ready to return home, stocked up with new clothes and a classy car. Sylvain: "We came back with a grey Jaguar that we bought for £300. We got it just to go to Kensington Market in, where we'd have tea, smoke hashish and buy boots all fucking day long. Remember the Mickey Mouse T-shirts, they were so popular? We brought a million of them back with us." Clothes and hash weren't their sole motive for visiting Europe: they needed a vacation from the things they couldn't change. While the more radical English hippies were incensed by the establishment's attempts to bring down the counter-culture by targeting the editors of the influential underground paper *OZ* and hauling them off to court to face obscenity charges, a far more real obscenity was being perpetrated against the young by the establishment in the USA.

The Vietnam war was raging and while old generals discussed strategies over the dinner table, the Vietnamese people were being massacred, and thousands of American sons were sent home in bodybags. The boys who would become the Dolls were of the atomic generation who endured nuclear air raid drills at school but were just young enough to avoid being drafted. Sylvain: "Vietnam was something that was just horrible going on around us. That war was screwed up, it was really the old against the young. Billy and me, we were so anti-establishment. I still wasn't a US citizen and neither was Billy."

One of the first recipients of a Kensington Market Mickey Mouse T-shirt was Johnny Genzale, with whom Sylvain and Billy had finally got on speaking terms when they returned to The States. When he first brought his bass down to jam with Syl and Billy, Johnny was particularly impressed by the stack of Marshall amps in the basement. Johnny Genzale was never meant to be a bass guitarist, he was jumpier than a kitten and far too erratic to pace anything evenly but Syl and Billy needed a bassist and wanted Johnny in their band. Nonetheless, Sylvain was pleased to pass on some of Mike Turby's musical methods. Sylvain: "When it really started between us three, we became like a family. Johnny started coming down to the basement and I taught him all the riffs I had learned from Mike and the things I had picked up on my own. I basically said, 'Look, if you know those scales and you go like this, instead of doing the whole fucking bar chord, just hold it with two fingers and you can make a little power chord.' Johnny took to that, baby! We'd all sit on the bed with these cheap guitars and do Marc Bolan songs, as well as some blues and instrumentals."

Sylvain, Billy and Johnny became the Dolls but they didn't get much further than the bed rehearsals before Syl nipped back to London to join Mercedes and Heidi Murcia, who were making sweaters and selling them to Kensington Market.

Johnny was already started on his routine of losing apartments on a regular basis and was crashing at the Chelsea Hotel after one too many dramatic fights with Janis, while a disregard for boring stuff like contributing to the rent had forced Gail Higgins Smith to ask him to move out of their East Village place. One evening as Johnny was hanging out on Bleecker Street, he noticed two very drunk and shady dudes in the process of trying to steal a motorbike, which was half hanging out the back of their battered Volkswagen van. When they suddenly dropped the bike and started towards him, he really wondered if he ought to run for it but his high platform boots were not designed for flight. As they drew closer he realised he'd seen them around at the Fillmore and Nobody's. Arthur: "I was with Rick Rivets when I saw him outside a pizza place. We were across the street and I said, 'Okay, here's that guy, why don't we go over and find out what's going on with him?' I went over and said, 'I hear you play guitar or bass or something, do you want to get together?' "

Rivets and Kane played lead and rhythm. When Johnny showed up the next afternoon, bass in hand, they thrashed around, checking out their musical compatibility. After a couple of weeks of rough rehearsals, Arthur gave Johnny the final go-ahead to take up the lead guitar. Arthur: "I was the one that promoted him from bass player to guitar player and put myself on bass because I knew that if I played bass with what he was playing on guitar, we would have something."

It was during this period of transformation that Johnny Genzale changed his surname, first to Volume, then settling on Thunders, after the DC cowboy comic book hero Johnny Thunder – Mystery Rider Of The Wild West. When a drummer called Ossie came on board, they rented a studio and riffed through a selection of Chuck Berry, Rolling Stones and Yardbirds covers. Ossie was swiftly replaced by Thunders' choice of drummer, Billy Murcia. Rick Rivets: "Billy was very wild, very up all the time. He had a lot of energy, he'd always be running around here and there. He'd always be dressed up, you never saw him look like crap. He'd always have his hair done and be wearing all the right clothes."

Once Billy was in the line-up, the action switched back to Queens. Arthur took a room in the Murcia's house and the band began rehearsing in the basement. This stage in the band's development is often referred to as their 'Actress' phase. Arthur: "We didn't really use the name Actress, it was just a suggestion by Johnny's girlfriend, Janis. It was all a part of the glitter thing, we had the first platform shoes and boots in New York because Billy's sister was in London and she knew where to get them. Also I had seen the Alice Cooper group, when they were all wearing silver jump suits and I knew we had to look wilder than that. We were the wildest looking people in New York, all we had to do was get some more clothes and we were set."

It became a drag for Thunders to keep lugging to Queens from the city every time the band got together, so they began looking for a rehearsal place in Manhattan. Off Columbus Avenue and 82nd Street they found a cycle shop with a couple of amps in the back whose owner, Rusty, was nicknamed 'Beanie' by the band on account of the funny little knitted caps that he wore. For their nightly rehearsals, Beanie would lock them inside the shop and to keep them going, Kane and Rivets would always pick up a quart of vodka which they split with Billy. Thunders, who steered clear of liquor, would provide pot and downers for everyone. He also brought in some of his own material and began to establish himself as the front man.

In October '71, Rick Rivets bought along a cassette player and recorded a typical Actress session, which was now almost entirely comprised of Thunders' numbers. 'That's Poison' is an undeveloped blueprint for 'Subway Train' featuring Johnny's near miss fretwork slipping and sliding all over the rails. All the downers and vodka had taken hold by the mournful 'I Am Confronted', an extended blues jam given some much needed structure by Murcia's insistent drumming.

Many years later, Thunders would rework 'Confronted' into the epic 'So Alone'. The foundation of 'It's Too Late' was also laid down with a Stonesy swagger that pre-empted the release of *Exile On Main Street*. 'Oh Dot', a Kane/Rivets composition, opens with catchy potential before collapsing through lack of support, while 'I'm A Boy, I'm A Girl' is reminiscent of Iggy Pop and James Willamson during their 'Kill City' period, minus the venom. 'Coconut Grove', also a Kane/Rivets effort, and 'Take Me To The Party' are a couple of good time rockers indebted to Chuck Berry but 'Why Am I Alone' reverts back to Johnny's melancholic tendencies with its drawn-out, sweeping guitars.

Although Thunders possessed a plaintive reedy voice that would have sufficed, he was more interested in being a lead guitarist than a front man. Rick Rivets: "Johnny wanted a singer. I don't know if he felt comfortable doing the vocals and playing. I remember we tried out one singer, he was wearing silver cowboy boots and a leather jacket, he was really terrible. Then David Johansen came down."

The connection with David Johansen was made through Rodrigo Soloman, a former tenant of the Murcia family, who moved into the city and took an apartment in the same building as David and his girlfriend Diane Poluski on East 6th Street. David Johansen: "There was a Colombian guy who lived in my building and he was friends with Billy and me. He told me that he knew these guys who were looking for a singer in their band. One day Billy and Arthur came to my door. I'm kind of exaggerating here, but Billy was like four feet tall and Arthur was eight feet tall and they both had these really high boots on and were kind of dressed like Marc Bolan. I just saw them standing there and liked them right away. I thought 'Oh God, this is great, what a pair of lunatics!' "

What Billy and Arthur saw was a lanky kid resembling the unlikely offspring of Mick Jagger and the French actress, Simone Signoret. In fact, David Roger Johansen was the product of a large working-class Catholic family from Staten Island, presided over by a Norwegian insurance salesman and his Irish wife. David grew up with a tantalising view of the New York City skyline that seemed to him like a stage set of miracles in which one day he would make a fabulous début. In the meantime he poured his frustration into a notebook, filling it with poems and lyrics. He began singing with a local outfit called The Vagabond Missionaries before graduating to Fast Eddie and The Electric Japs, an art rock band who actually made it to the city, doing support slots and playing small gigs at The Cafe Wha and Cafe au Go Go in Greenwich Village.

David would later pep up his past by telling journalists he had appeared in a couple of skin flicks prior to joining the Dolls, specifically *Bike Boys Go Ape* and *Studs On Main Street*, but this was merely an early indication of Johansen's irreverent sense of humour that got taken too seriously. David Johansen had been around the same circuit as the rest of the boys that became Dolls, the only difference being that his taste in music had more of a soul edge. David: "I've always liked a lot of different kinds of music, R&B, Cuban and Puerto Rican. I liked Howard Tate a lot, he was a soul singer with a short career, he OD'd on heroin. I liked Otis Redding and Archie Bell and The Drells 'cos they had a really good sense of humour. As a kid, I followed Janis Joplin, I was big on her from when I was 16 until she died. I used to go a long way to see her sing. In 1969 I went to San Francisco and stayed in Berkeley. I used to go to the Fillmore West and see all the bands that came into town. In New York I used to go to the Fillmore East practically every night in the late Sixties, early Seventies."

Pursuing his interest in drama, Johansen gravitated to the artistic underground and landed a small part as a spear carrier in one of Charles Ludlum's avant garde Ridiculous Theatre productions. He then met and moved in with a former model, Diane Poluski, who was several years his senior. Part of the Andy Warhol scene, Diane Poluski had played Holly Wood-lawn's pregnant sister in *Trash* and introduced David to some of the main participant's in the world of Warhol. Whereas Johnny, Billy, Arthur and Rick liked to soak up the rock ambience at Nobody's bar, Johansen preferred the company of the art and drag crowd at Max's Kansas City. Social tastes aside, once Johansen had trekked to Rusty Beanie's, where he roared his way through a couple of covers and wrapped his lascivious lips around a harmonica, the band knew they'd found their singer. The Dolls moniker was reactivated and Arthur tagged on the New York prefix. Arthur: "I wanted to add the 'New York' because in New York you would always be hearing on the radio and television like . . . New York Jets, New York Yankees, New York Vets, New York this and that . . . and I thought we'd get an immediate local following if we called ourselves The New York Dolls, and also it sounded like something from a 1930's Broadway show."

The final link in the chain happened when Sylvain returned from Europe at the end of 1971. He found a very different band to the one he left behind and was put out that they were calling themselves The New York Dolls, the name he'd first seen on the sign above the toy hospital. Sylvain: "I got upset at that and gave them a little bit of my French 'cos I was pissed off. It was a fucking groovy name and I wanted to have it."

Once he'd cooled off and returned to speaking English, Sylvain began to jam with the band on a fairly regular basis although he missed out on The New York Dolls' rowdy début as the dance band at a city sponsored beggar's banquet. The welfare workers in charge of The Endicott Hotel, a crumbling refuge for the homeless across the street from Rusty Beanies, had organised a Christmas party for the impoverished Endicott residents. The group originally booked to play cancelled at the last minute but an enterprising member of the welfare committee stopped on the street to listen to the late night racket coming from the cycle shop and approached the band. On Christmas eve, Johnny, David, Billy, Arthur and Rick dragged their equipment over the icy road and set up in the decaying ballroom of The Endicott. The city's welfare department picked up the tab on a sudden surge of electricity as The New York Dolls plugged in and got the audience dancing to a vintage jukebox's worth of R&B covers.

Rick Rivets had always looked on being in the band as casual fun, a cool excuse to get bombed and make some noise with the guys. He had no expectations for them beyond Rusty's and a couple more gigs on the same low level as their Endicott début. Rivets: "I thought it was just a lark 'cos no bands from New York ever got signed. I thought you had to be real professional, great guitar players. Me and Arthur, we didn't have any idea about being in a band."

While Arthur was most certainly a disconnected character with little real knowledge of the music business, as were the rest of the Dolls really, he was sure that he wanted to stay in the band. Kane had a private chat with Thunders. Rick had started to skip rehearsals and was rumoured to be playing with another outfit anyway. Johnny: "Rick Rivets started fucking around, coming to practise late and stuff like that, so we canned him and got Sylvain in."

Rivets departure thus allowed Sylvain to swan back into the line-up and take his rightful place as a New York Doll.

2

The Babylon Beat Goes On

The Manhattan night time playground where the New York Dolls came of age was a great deal more decadent in the Seventies than it is today. The dark was illuminated by neon and a supporting cast of thousands who shunned daylight hours – the superflys and their hard-eyed whores, slum kids, hustlers, junkies, chickenhawks, runaways, winos, street punks and criminals fluttered like moths around the X-rated fairy lights. The Big Apple's artistic community took the pulse of a city bordering on moral and financial bankruptcy and acted out accordingly, creating an ambience comparable to Berlin before the second world war broke up the party.

New York has always enjoyed a strong sub-culture, from the glittering drag balls of the Thirties that were celebrated in *The Young And Evil* (Charles Henri Ford & Parker Tyler) to the artists and writers who made Greenwich Village their home. The most relevant contemporary artist to play a part in The New York Dolls' story was Andy Warhol, both in person and for the scene he created. By the time the Dolls hit the city, however, Warhol was distancing himself from the original Factory freak clique that he'd cultivated in the Sixties and relocating to the expensive Upper East Side. This was largely the result of Valerie Solanis's assassination attempt but although Warhol now moved with the wealthy, conservative uptown set, his influence remained omnipresent in his former realm. The outrageous drag queens, Holly Woodlawn, Candy Darling and the trash-glam Jackie Curtis, all of whom had appeared in Warhol's movies, remained as permanent fixtures in the notorious red-walled backroom of Max's Kansas City.

Located in Union Square at the bottom end of Park Avenue South, Max's was close to the Factory and still the social centre of the Warhol set and thus, by association, the centre of New York's Underground universe.

In the summer of 1970, The Velvet Underground played their final shows at Max's. When the Velvet's disbanded, the disaffected habituees of downtown New York lost their voice for no other group had so chillingly chronicled their lives and vices. Lou Reed sang about heroin and S&M. Nico, the funereal chanteuse that Warhol introduced to their ranks, mourned for each and every subject she intoned.

Before The Velvet Underground's subterranean domination, New York's musical history was steeped in the great rock'n'roll boom of the fifties. Those New York groups who might have been looked upon as near contemporaries of The Velvets were not particularly representative of the city. The Young Rascals, The Lovin' Spoonful and Vanilla Fudge all reached some level of international success but they spoke more for the time they came from rather than the place. New York never had a localised scene or anyone to narrate the musical rush of the city until Andy Warhol and The Velvet Underground but by 1971, they had abdicated. By 1972, all eyes were on The New York Dolls to take the crown. Soon, they would go far beyond The Velvet Underground's dark, introverted predilections to become the extroverted oracles of Manhattan.

First it was Johnny and Janis who moved into the loft on 119 Chrystie Street, above the Chinese noodle factory. They were soon followed by Billy and Sylvain. Because there was just floor space and no rooms aside from a couple of wall closets and a separate bathroom, Johnny, Billy and Syl, like a surreal Boy Scout troop, pitched ex-army tents in the loft for a semblance of individual privacy. Fortunately, they weren't reduced to cooking over an indoor campfire, having managed to fashion a kitchen out of scrap salvaged from the City's garbage dump. They dined frequently on the proceeds of shoplifting sprees, aided and abetted by Heidi Murcia who had a knack for chicken and potato theft. Once a month, before the landlord came knocking, the boys would throw a rent party. Rehearsing at Rusty's had accustomed them to playing in a confined space. Sylvain: "One of Johnny's friends would be at the door collecting $2 from each person that arrived. Janis was in charge of the lights. We performed in the kitchen area 'cos it was a step or two up, behind us was the refrigerator and the sink. There would be guys selling drugs and girls selling sex and we'd play rock'n'roll. 'Human Being' and 'Frankenstein' came from one of those long, rent party nights."

In place of party snacks, the band would consume a form of cheap powdered acid known as belladonna, which was rolled up in a cigarette paper then gulped down. It's no wonder that the hulking nightmare of 'Frankenstein', which was sired by Sylvain and David, came to life under such chemically addled circumstances. Sylvain: "It's about your lover being a monster. That monster could be anything that is taboo or experimental." Johansen's lyrical take – "Well I'm asking you as a person/Is it a crime/Is it a crime/For you to fall in love with a Frankenstein/Is it wrong/Could it be wrong, wrong/Baby don't you want a friend?" – is that of an impassioned advocate for the grotesque. Insulated by an ominous bass run and panic stricken drumming, the guitars whoosh in like scythes. Although able to carry the 'Frankenstein' riff through a stoned rent party, Thunders faltered when it came to working up the song in rehearsal. Sylvain: "Johnny said it had too many chords. If you introduced a song with more than A, E and G you had big problems 'cos he didn't want to cross that line. It would always be 'Sylvain, can we talk about this? There's six chords in this song.' I'd say 'Yeah, but it goes over and over again. Just hold the notes, okay.' We'd go back and he'd either do speed repetitive stuff or he'd come in with lots of little riffs."

'Human Being' developed into an incredibly honest assessment of the foibles and frailties that exist in everyone and excuses them all. "If I'm acting like a king/Well that's 'cos I'm a human being/And if I want too many things/Don't you know well/I'm a human being/And if I've got to dream/Baby, baby, I'm a human being/And when it get's a bit obscene/Whoaa I'm a human being. . . ." Bouyed along on a bouncing rhythm section, Thunders' attack is sharper than a tatooist's needle making its mark but the outline is coloured by Sylvain.

Another song that took its first steps in the loft was 'Jet Boy'. Sylvain: "Johnny was playing the opening riff and I said 'Wait a minute' and did my little baby chords which was a D and a G. We jammed it at rehearsal and David said he had some great lyrics for it. Then we added the background oohs and ahhs." The Dolls were all Jet Boys, cartoon kids of the jet age, flying around New York. Although he'd just turned 19, Johansen had absorbed the beat generation literature of Allen Ginsberg and Jack Kerouac and was developing into an astute lyricist with a gift for wry social observation.

As in every band, a pecking order started to establish itself within the Dolls. Johansen's dominant personality and Thunders' needy ego brought them to the fore. Sylvain baulked at the idea of always being the rhythm guitarist and vied to share the soloing with Johnny, while Johansen's role as group spokesman was largely self-appointed (though he *was* the most articulate member of the group). As yet the divisions were so minuscule they hardly registered in the overall picture of the hottest, cutest gang in town. Theirs was a sublime combination: from the verbose, theatrical front man flanked by a beautiful bad boy lead guitarist to the sexy imp on rhythm, an oddball automaton on bass and the wild thing at the back beating drums. David: "There is only about seven or eight kinds of people in the world so when you get five of them and they are all individuals in a group, it's good. Everybody had a fully formed character, everybody loved rock'n'roll. Rock'n'roll had a profound influence on our alienation. For certain kids, when you're 15, life sucks, then all of a sudden you get rock'n'roll and you realise that life can be good, we all felt that about rock'n'roll. When we got together that was our bond, that was what we talked about. We had different influences but we threw them all together."

On May 29, 1972, The New York Dolls played their second date in the Palm Room of the Diplomat Hotel, where The Pox had débuted. Adjacent to the Times Square porn palaces and peep shows, the Diplomat gig was organised in conjunction with the Warhol crew and featured Jackie Curtis in a support slot. At the bottom of the bill was a band called Shaker, whose drummer, Jerry Nolan, rather impressed Billy. The event, advertised as an 'Invitation Beyond The Valley', garnered a couple of lousy reviews in the theatrical sections of local papers. Some of the Dolls' very early appearances baffled critics who were unsure as to whether they were a theatrical troupe, a rock act or both.

The Dolls got to know Jackie Curtis, who had been immortalised in song by Lou Reed when he wrote 'Walk On The Wild Side'. Curtis, who appeared in Andy Warhol's *Flesh* as well as numerous self-penned plays, was an integral Underground figure, but like so many from that scene, had drifted into using hard drugs. During an afternoon soiree with Jackie, initiated by David, Sylvain caught the sharp end of the stick. Sylvain: "Jackie was like 'Hey, I can't get this needle between my fingers, would you help me?' I was such a naïve schmuck, it's such a sexual thing to help someone fix, it's penetrative and that's why Jackie wanted me to help."

The Dolls did their next two dates, once again with Jackie Curtis supporting, in the steamy setting of a gay bath house in Brooklyn. Arthur: "We did these very weird shows with Jackie at these baths. It was like there was no audience because all the guys stayed in their cubicles having sex with someone, so we didn't know what to do. Everyone in the group had taken MDA, I think I was selling it at the time. It was kind of like LSD without the heavy thinking but it makes you stumble around, hallucinating. We weren't sure how to dress for the bath house, so the first night we went feminine, I wore hot pants. They didn't seem to appreciate the femme look, although we had a lot of fun on the MDA. The next night we came back in leather and chains and got more interest, everyone came out of their little cubicles to watch us."

Like Arthur, Johnny Thunders also made a few extra bucks selling pot and acid but it was Syl and Billy who came up with a ruse that provided the band with some much needed extra equipment. Most of their guitars had been bought through a local paper called *Buy-Line* that specialised in second-hand goods, advertised by the owners. Billy and Sylvain got used to browsing and pouting at all the instruments they couldn't afford in the music shops dotted around Greenwich Village, until the day they walked into a store that boasted the cheapest guitars in town. Hanging on the wall, right in front of them was an old bass of Johnny's that had been ripped off. The dandy duo sussed that the owner was acquiring hot goods and after some coercion Billy got the bass back. Then Sylvain spied a tantalising Les Paul cutaway for sale and memorised the serial number. Sylvain: "Me and Billy forged a receipt with the serial number of the guitar we wanted and antiqued it up a bit. We had a hippy philosophy – if you are going to steal, you steal from the crooks. A couple of hours later we went back and I gave the store owner the forged receipt. Very grudgingly he hands over the guitar. I go, 'What about the case?' He goes, 'They didn't give me no fucking case. Get out of here.' "

With the accumulation of equipment, the Dolls began to search out less obscure venues than they'd previously played. In a place like New York, it should have been a cinch. David: "When I was a high school kid, there were tons of clubs in New York, on MacDougal Street, Bleecker Street and millions of bands playing in the Village. It was a really rocking scene, but then for some reason, about the time we got started, the whole place had been boarded up, it was kind of like a disaster area. I don't know what happened, it was just gone and there was no place to play rock'n'roll."

Janis Cafasso took the initiative to scout around for an appropriate locale where The New York Dolls could establish themselves. She came up with a theatre complex one block west of Broadway called the Mercer Arts Center. Attached to the Broadway Central Hotel, a building that had seen its glory days way back in the 1890s, the Mercer Arts Center was the brainchild of Art Kaback, an air conditioning mogul with a love of theatre. The centre housed different sized theatres named after various authors and playwrights, including Oscar Wilde and George Bernard Shaw, while the overall decor had A *Clockwork Orange* feel. Millions had been poured into the venture but aside from an experimental video workshop and a reasonably successful run of *One Flew Over The Cuckoo's Nest*, the Mercer was losing money. The New York Dolls were not what the centre's booking agent, Mark Lewis, would have considered 'culture' but they needed to get people through the door. Lewis designated the Mirror Room, a tiny space in the back of the arts centre, for the forthcoming gig which was advertised as 'the Dolls of N.Y'.

While Janis got busy ringing up everybody from close friends to interested acquaintances and approachable journalists, the band put in some practice on their ever developing set. Tired of the nightly lock-ins at Rusty Beanies, they had moved to Talent-Recon, a more convenient rehearsal place managed by a fire-eater called Satan, who dressed accordingly, bar a forked tail. The Dolls were hardly proficient at their craft but they managed to take advantage of their shortcomings by playing an imaginative approximation of rock'n'roll that gave their music a sharply dyslexic signature. Thunders' guitar sound bucked and whinnied like a wild pony and Kane had his own unique bass technique. David: "A lot of the Dolls' sound I attribute to Arthur's bass playing and it made us sound really strange, and different from other rock bands. He couldn't breath and play at the same time, so he would take a really deep breath, play a lot of notes and then take another deep breath and start playing again."

Down at Talent-Recon they sweated over 'Black Girl', a song of lust penned as always by Johansen – "A new black girl/Moved in on my block/I gave her my key/Said you don't have to knock/I said c'mon you got what I need/Why don't you c'mon and don't you make my heart bleed . . ." Johansen's throaty, foghorn vocals could have been heard clearly from another city, never mind the block into which the new girl had moved. He cajoles, he pleads, he even offers her money – "20 dollar bill says you can keep the change/All you gotta do is step back in on my range . . ." – all to no avail. Throbbing bass and a truly horny guitar charge pushes forward a number that would soon be retitled 'Bad Girl'.

Right from the start, the Dolls incorporated into their set covers that reflected their affinity with rhythm and blues. However, they didn't just pick any old foot stomping tune, preferring instead numbers with a dramatic story line and a sense of humour that could be acted out. Gamble and Huff's 'Showdown', recorded by Archie Bell and The Drells, concerns a challenge at a street gang dance contest. Sonny Boy Williamson's 'Don't Start Me Talking' also received The New York Dolls' treatment. Casting Johansen as the bitchy madam who just won't stop with the gossip, the band turned the song into a cacophonous cat-fight, pinioned by their front man's foaming harmonica.

Spending time at Talent-Recon brought the Dolls into further contact with the members of Shaker, who also rehearsed there, as well as a blue jean clad cowboy band who plugged away fruitlessly night after night. After seeing the Dolls' career begin to take off, the cowboy band started making up like animals and playing under the name of Kiss.

Another band shacked up at Talent-Recon with a slightly higher public profile was Eric Emerson and The Magic Tramps. Emerson, who resembled a child's picture book angel, had been a dancer in Andy Warhol's live multimedia event The Exploding Plastic Inevitable. He also dated girls from the Factory and had just separated from Elda Gentile, with whom he had a young son, Branch. Elda was watching the baby when a friend told her that a fabulous new band was playing at her ex-old man's rehearsal place, so she went to check them out. Elda: "It was the Dolls. I was totally blown away by their music, it was straight forward don't give a shit rock'n'roll. At the time, all you'd hear on the radio was Jimi Hendrix, Janis Joplin and The Doors. The music industry was cashing in on all the Sixties legends. There was nothing else happening. Then, all of a sudden, here was this band who were having the time of their lives. And they were all gorgeous. I absolutely loved the band and noticed that a lot of other girls that were around them loved them too." Elda invited Sylvain to sample her authentic Italian cooking and shortly afterwards he gave up his tent and moved into her top floor, First Avenue apartment.

In early June, The New York Dolls played their first gig at the Mercer Arts Center, supporting Satan the fire eater and The Magic Tramps. David Johansen later told *Circus* magazine that . . . "It all came together at the Mercer Arts Center. We were opening for The Magic Tramps, but we were so good that they booed The Tramps off stage, so we opened and closed the concert." The show couldn't have gone better for the Dolls had it been a scene in an old Hollywood musical where the struggling starlets captivate Broadway. The audience were enraptured and couldn't wait to tell their friends, while the arts centre booked the band for a second show, this time in the larger Oscar Wilde room. The little buzz of interest around the Dolls swiftly grew into a storm of excitement. Although the staff at the Mercer Arts Center didn't much like the look of the Dolls or the freaky crowd they attracted, it was worth it for the profit made at the bar in the foyer every time the band played.

On June 13, the Dolls kicked off a 17-week, Tuesday night residency in the Oscar Wilde Room. With several floor-to-ceiling mirrors that reflected the band from all angles, and an audience capacity of 200, it was a perfect setting, one that Dorian Gray himself might even have envied. The fact that it was housed in so pleasant a location as an arts centre made it more attractive to the Max's Kansas City crowd, who with their social skittishness might not have been so willing to attend had the Dolls been playing in a seedy little rock dive. Gail Higgins Smith: "The Mercer Arts Center was very upmarket, with seats and theatre lighting. When the Dolls started playing there, they brought together the music and art scene. Suddenly the outrageousness of the art world, which was basically Andy Warhol's scene, and the music world started rubbing off on each other. At the time I was working in a straight department store with these two guys who called themselves the Tois sisters, one of them was the heir to the Heinz fortune. The next Dolls' gig I went to, Heinz Tois showed up in a dress. Now, I hadn't even mentioned the band or the gig to him, and there he was in a dress, that's how influential the Dolls were starting to get."

The New York Dolls' audiences were almost as much of an event as the band's onstage performances. The group gave free licence for everybody to be themselves, whatever their persuasion. Sylvain: "Tuesdays were our night, and boy everyone would come to see us. It was like a party. At the beginning there was a mixture of people we knew from Nobody's and the drag queen crowd. It wasn't quite a circus but it was definitely freaky. There was one guy, me and Johnny named him 'Clothes Tits' 'cos he'd always wear an open, shiny black vest and he'd have clothes pins on his nipples. There was a couple of Tibetan girls covered in all kinds of tribal tattoos, one of whom became Billy's girlfriend. All the drag queens had glitter in their beards and wore lipstick. The umbrella man dressed up in nothing but discarded umbrellas that he'd found on the street and there was 'Flop Top' who covered himself with the ring-pulls of soda and beer cans." The wild happenings that the Baltimore film maker John Waters was creating in his mondo-bizarre features at the time, like *Multiple Maniacs* and *Pink Flamingos*, The New York Dolls and their fans were living.

All the gender bending that was going on around the Dolls seemed to affect David Johansen most of all. It may not have been entirely in jest that he told the band he wanted to be the first male rock star to have breast implants; after all, Candy Darling's had looked fabulous. Johansen's pronouncement was greeted by a hail of giggles from the rest of the boys. When cornered on his sexuality, David pronounced himself "trisexual", meaning he'd try anything. The New York Dolls were predominantly heterosexual, even though the hothouse atmosphere in which they bloomed did encourage one or two little same sex dalliances. It was never their intention, not at the outset anyway, to be perceived as a fag rock band. They were pretty peacocks, not chicks with dicks, who wanted to dress to the limit. It was their lead singer, who had taken to calling himself David Jo, that took it over the line, into camp, hands-on-hip posturing.

Sylvain: "It wasn't until we got David that we became really flamboyant but he took it to a level that I was never happy with. I'd worn make-up before his arrival, and Johnny used to wear girl's shoes all the time but we never thought of it as, 'Hey, we're going to dress up as women.' We weren't trying to turn men on by looking like women, except maybe for David 'cos that's the way he played it. I said to David, 'Are you gay, do you want to be a transvestite' but he would never give me a proper answer and I remember saying to him, 'If you are that's cool, but you shouldn't play around with something if it isn't for real.'" One of the earliest and least salacious rumours circulated about the band concerned an attempt by them to gain entrance into The Barbizon, a women-only hotel in Midtown, with the punch line being that Thunders was the only Doll refused admission at the door.

Speculation about The New York Dolls was reaching a gossip-worthy level, and they knew they had truly arrived when Ed McCormack, a reporter from Andy Warhol's *Interview* magazine, showed up to do an article on them. The result was a glowing piece that stacked up the band's credentials even higher by mentioning that Lou Reed had been to see them and thought they were 'very cute'. McCormack concluded that . . . "Onstage in the Oscar Wilde Room they generate a futuristic energy that gets people up off their asses and dancing. The lead singer, who looks like Mick Jagger's skinny kid sister, stands there all knock-kneed and plaintive, throwing his arms out palms-up in a gesture of helpless horny adolescent frustration and growling and moaning in this surprisingly gruff voice, singing these great teenage torture-rack blues-rock sock-hop type of rock and roll songs about how he has personality problems and no one else understands, and the lead guitarist with the green-streaked hair and the hermaphrodite leg is leaning into the mike to back him up with the harmony on vocals, and the drummer is pounding away, and the big tall skinny goldylocked blond bassist is looking a little shy in his lipstick and pink pantyhose . . . the Dolls have been getting a lot of people in New York up off their decadent asses and making them dance."

Once Uncle Lou had given the band his blessing, various other daring celebrities came to check them out at the Mercer Arts Center, including Bette Midler, former Velvet John Cale and Alice Cooper. The fashion model Cindy Lang, who was Alice Cooper's girlfriend, began an affair with Johnny, while Cooper's manager, Shep Gordon, showed an interest in taking care of the Dolls' career. It could've been a great combination but David Jo and Johnny believed that trickery was afoot, and that all Gordon wanted to do was sign them and shelve them because they were a threat to the Alice Cooper group. Rod Stewart's manager, Billy Gaff, also made the Dolls a serious management offer, but all bets were cancelled after he got them a gig supporting Long John Baldry in a club out on Long Island. Gaff even sent a limousine over to take the band to Long Island. Alas, they had been guzzling belladonna and liquor, and were in no fit state to do anything other than slump in the back of the car. Murcia was sick and they arrived too late to do the show.

The next key piece of press covering the Dolls' career this

far, came through *Melody Maker*'s New York correspondent, Roy Hollingworth, who viewed their scene like an intrepid reporter in some hitherto undiscovered, yet exotic continent – hardly surprising in view of Hollingworth's background as a reporter on the *Derby Evening Telegraph*. The enterprising *Melody Maker*, then England's most influential rock mag, was the only London music weekly to have a full time staff reporter covering the New York rock scene, and Hollingworth was the first of its London based reporters to be given the job. Of course, he needed a photographer to capture the wildlife in Shangri-la. Leee Black Childers was recommended to Hollingworth by Lillian Roxon, the mother of all female rock writers. Originally from Louisville, Kentucky, Childers was like peaches in brandy, luscious and sharp. He was just about to be recruited by David Bowie and Tony De Frie's management company MainMan, having first come to their attention in London while stage managing *Pork* at the Roundhouse in 1971. The play, based on Andy Warhol's phone conversations, and featuring Wayne County, gave David Bowie his first introduction to the New York underground.

Roy Hollingworth wanted to be the first to introduce English music fans to The New York Dolls. With Leee in tow, he made his way to the Chrystie Street loft. Sylvain: "Roy Hollingworth told us he'd seen us the week before at The Mercer Arts Center, and that he thought we'd been fabulous so we talked to him, then Leee decided he wanted to take a photograph of us in Johnny's closet, so we've got all these clothes around us. There was so much love going on between us at that point, it was really groovy." Leee's photo of the band, whose painted and pouting faces look almost too big for their skinny bodies, became a b&w minor classic.

In a matter of weeks, the Dolls effortlessly clambered up the social ladder. Once they reached the clouds, Andy Warhol began courting them. Leee Black Childers: "They'd go to parties with Andy, and be outrageously gorgeous painted boys, dressed a little like girls. He would go to Gloria Vanderbilt's for a dinner party, and she'd announce his arrival, and he'd waltz in with David on one arm and Johnny or Sylvain on the other and they'd have their lipstick on and play the role. Syl was very thin and very pretty, he wore a lot of ruffles and chiffon, he had the body for it, too, 'cos he's so small and cute. He was just like an ornament. Andy loved being shocking and so did the Dolls. I don't think they understood just how shocking they were, but Andy did and that's why he would take them to sit-down dinner parties, where people like Gloria Vanderbilt would have to be polite to them."

The summer of '72 was particularly hot and so were The New York Dolls. They were the season's favourite accessories, lauded and applauded wherever they roamed. Arthur never had to buy another drink, Johnny was given pills like they were candy and Billy was left wanting for neither. Syl got to compare stretch pants with Rudolph Nureyev while David Jo got to live out the scenes he'd dreamed of back on Staten Island. Leee Black Childers: "There was this great party held in a hotel suite. Mick Jagger, David Bowie, Bette Midler and this actor, Hiram Keller, a friend of mine, were all there. Hiram had appeared in Fellini's *Satyricon*, he was openly gay but the thing he loved even more than fucking was scandalising. Now, David Johansen liked to flirt. He did a lot of public hugging and kissing, although most of it was just for show. Hiram took David into the bathroom and locked the door. They could have just been in there giggling, but all of us saw the two of them go in there, and not come out again for half an hour."

For all the uptown revelry, the Dolls preferred their own funky territory, where no one had to wait to be announced. Arthur: "The downtown Dolls met everybody from uptown, at some point. Then we all decided that the Dolls should stay downtown and they could stay uptown." The band set up camp in the back room of Max's Kansas City, but their presence in the throne room of the Underground ruffled some people's feather boas. For those who haunted the shadows of their long lost youth, The New York Dolls were a threat. To others they were just upstart Nobody's kids. Leee Childer's roommate, Wayne County, whom *16* magazine described as 'a drag-rock Lenny Bruce' was the club DJ. Wayne: "When Johnny used to walk in with all his hair teased up, he'd get called 'Wig city'. I used to think of him being more like Ronnie Ronnette and that he was one of the people from Nobody's. We were Max's people and when a Nobody's person walked in, we'd say, 'Oh, Nobody just walked in'."

Before long, most of the backroom's patrons adapted to the Dolls, and some even adopted them. Sylvain: "We were their babies, we were cute, we had style and they knew it." Wayne County in particular formed an alliance with the Dolls, who championed his own band, Queen Elizabeth. The most sought-after spot in the back room was the round table, where only the club's elite got to gather. Wayne: "You fought for the round table, and if you got it, you had to be able to hold it. Well, one night the Dolls had taken it over, and there were all these people sitting around. Billy was wearing make-up, and over high heels and tight pants, he was wearing a dress, which was what the Dolls were famous for doing at the time, putting a dress on, over whatever they were wearing. Some girl started screaming at him 'FAGGOT! You fucking QUEER!' Billy had a temper, he would freak. That night he went crazy, he stood up, cleared the whole table, took the salad dish and threw it at the girl, then the glasses, then a bottle. Then he tipped the table over, the whole back room turned into something out of a Western brawl scene. It was incredible." The resulting chaos did not endear the band to Mickey Ruskin, the usually liberal owner of Max's. Billy and Sylvain were later barred from the club after they were caught smoking cocaine in the bathroom.

The only consistency in the Dolls' lives was their residency at The Mercer Arts Center. Although a couple of their Tuesday night slots were disrupted by anti-transvestite, lesbian and gay demonstrators who gathered at the entrance of the Arts Center to protest over the 'transvestite scum' playing inside. Wayne County was also similarly targetted when he performed at NYU. The Mercer Arts Center had made the concession of allowing the Dolls the use of a bathroom as a backstage/dressing area. Pushing his way through the small, packed room that had turned into an aftershow party, came a man in his thirties, keen to locate the band.

Sylvain: "He was wearing a safari suit and he looked kind of weird standing next to these guys with glitter in their beards. Then he comes up to us and says, 'I don't know if I've just seen the best band in the world or the worst.' That was Marty Thau's introduction."

3
Too Hot To Handle

Marty Thau had been out on the town with his wife, Betty, celebrating his decision to resign as the head of A&R at Paramount records. While this kind of career move would make most folks anxious, Marty, or the 'Mighty Thau' as he was known in the music business, was feeling upbeat. He had a solid gold reputation forged on an instinct for potential. After an apprenticeship as an executive trainee at *Billboard* magazine, he took a job at the newly formed Cameo Parkway records, and became part of a team behind 28 hit records in one year. Then he moved on to Buddah records and repeated the Midas routine with a string of succesful singles, including 'Yummy Yummy Yummy', 'Oh Happy Day' and 'Green Tambourine'. He then sold Van Morrison's *Astral Weeks* and *Moondance* albums to Warner Brothers before starting the short stint at Paramount. His next project was already taking shape. Maurice Levy, who had amassed a considerable fortune through music publishing and Roulette Records, had just offered to finance a singles-only label if Thau would run it for him.

After dinner, Marty and Betty took a walk through the Village, where they spotted a tiny flyer advertising The New York Dolls. Thau had already been tipped off about the band by some of his business buddies, and decided to follow the lead to the Mercer Arts Center. While he enjoyed the Dolls' set, he was aware of their shortcomings but not unduly concerned. Marty: "They were so entertaining, so visual, so animated and full of life but on the other hand, they were almost out of tune. They weren't playing that good but it almost didn't seem to matter. We got to the door to leave, when I said, 'Let's go back, I want to talk to these guys.' I liked their songs and they sounded commercial. It crossed my mind that maybe they could be the first group that I could sign to the singles label. I went backstage, met them and we agreed to get together a couple of weeks later, at Max's Kansas City."

For all their bravura, the only real career advance made thus far by the Dolls had been the addition of a sound man and general all round helper, Peter Jordan. A local boy who'd played in countless bands living the hand-to-mouth existence of a struggling musician, Jordan was friendly with Barbara Troiani, a seamstress who spent most of her time customising and repairing the Dolls' flimsy threads. Following a year in Vermont, gigging with a bar band, Jordan was hungry for some New York news. Barbara Troiani sent him straight to the Mercer Arts Center. A sociable, together kind of guy, Peter got talking to the band after they soundchecked and wound up working with them. Peter: "I was a little more technically orientated and I told them I thought they could sound better so I started doing their sound for them. They were a lazy bunch of sods, so it was easy to drift into doing everything because they wouldn't do nothing. I started making ten bucks a night and it just kind of grew from there."

As well as attracting the art and drag crowd, The New York Dolls also drew in kids from Queens, The Bronx and Brooklyn who began to root for the band like a home team. Yet for all their new-found adulation, the shy lead guitarist had only just started to play facing the audience. Cyrinda Foxe, a beautiful blonde Warhol ingenue who'd appeared in the NY production of *Pork*, was turned on to the Dolls by Leee Black Childers. "They started to get a young following, all these kids from the Boroughs would come in to see them but Johnny wouldn't face the audience. Eventually he turned around and took off like a rocket. All the girls went mad for him." Andy Warhol was keen for Cyrinda to marry a wealthy uptown boy but Miss Foxe rebelled and started to date David Jo. Cyrinda: "Andy wanted to marry me off to a banker but I was still young, 19 or 20. I'd only just got out of the house so why go back in? I thought David was the funniest person, he was intelligent, well read. He wasn't pretty or handsome, he was kooky. As an artist I thought he was brilliant, he knew politics and he knew society. Much to the chagrin of the whole uptown Warhol crowd, I started going out with him."

As arranged that night at the Arts Center, the Dolls met with Marty Thau in the backroom of Max's and like delinquents on a first date they were somewhat better behaved than usual. Marty: "I was impressed with their clarity as to how they were going to become a big rock'n'roll group. They were very confident, very funny and very intelligent. Over the next few weeks we spoke even further and I decided to hell with it, I'm not going to waste this group just for a single. I'd like to get involved with them on a much broader scale, so I presented them with the idea of management. We spent time discussing it and it was decided that I'd be their manager." While Marty had a golden reputation and a comfortable lifestyle, he didn't have any ready cash available to sink into the band but he did have the phone number of two booking agents from the world renowned William Morris agency who had set up on their own.

It's hard to imagine that Steve Leber and David Krebs weren't born sucking on cigars and clutching contracts for their parents to sign, so deeply ingrained are they in show-biz tradition. Peter Jordan: "Leber and Krebs were strictly attracted to one thing, the potential for lucre. I got along with Leber and Krebs, but they are both sharks in the the true showbiz sense. Marty isn't a shark, he's more like a dolphin." When Thau had been at Paramount, Leber and Krebs had suggested that some form of business alliance might be mutually beneficial. Marty invited them to see the Dolls and they went straight for the bait. Steve Leber: "I, like everyone else, thought they were outrageous. They were different from anything I had seen before. Having been at the William Morris agency, I knew what mainstream rock was, I'd been the Rolling Stones' booking agent for a long time."

Marty proposed that he would act as The New York Dolls' personal manager while Leber and Krebs would deal with their financial and contractual affairs. Aside from taking care of the Dolls, Leber and Krebs acted as booking agents for Argent and B.B. King and were also responsible for the *Jesus Christ Superstar* touring company. Out of the managerial trinity now working on behalf of the Dolls, David Krebs had the least input because he was spending time with their other new signing, Aerosmith. Both The New York Dolls and Aerosmith were placed on the starting block by the same people at the same time. Arthur: "It's almost like they had one of those gentlemen's bets for a dollar. David Krebs had Aerosmith, Steve Leber had the Dolls. It feels like they said, 'We'll give them each two years to see how they do, then we'll pull the plug on the least happening band.' "

While the contracts were being drawn up, Marty whisked the Dolls into Blue Rock studios in the Soho area for an evening's recording. Later released as *The Mercer St. Sessions* because it reproduced a typical Oscar Wilde Room set of the time, the recording was never meant to be used for anything other than as reference tapes by the band. Rootsy versions of 'Human Being', 'Frankenstein', 'Bad Girl' and 'Jet Boy' were solidly nailed next to a couple of newer compositions. 'Personality Crisis' tells a tale of social schizophrenia, wonderfully scripted by Johansen: "You're a prima ballerina on a spring afternoon/Change into the wolfman/You're howling at the moon . . ." Like a wheelchair hijack, the jolting rhythm section and scraping guitars barely avoid collision. 'Looking For A Kiss' pitches teenage desire against those angels of doom that are more interested in hard drugs than sex. A down and dirty revision of Marc Bolan's 'Get It On' keeps the blood pumping while David vents his frustrations: "I didn't come here lookin' for no fix, ah uh-uh no!/I been out all night in the rain babe/Just looking for a kiss . . ." Aside from 'Don't Start Me

Talking', the boys also did a cute cover of Parker, Floyd and Cropper's 'Don't Mess With Cupid' and put to bed a rocking remake of Bo Diddley's 'Pills'. At the time, Bo Diddley was out on the road, playing a string of club dates. After one of their gigs, the Dolls rushed to Long Island, eager to catch Mr Diddley in action. Sylvain: "We were all next to the stage, dressed the way we dressed and we're all yelling for 'Pills' and he's shaking his head at us. Every time there's a break between songs we keep yelling 'Pills' at him. It appeared that he'd forgotten the song, and then he goes, 'I think these kids over here want drugs, if anyone's got any, these guys want them!' We left and later on he reintroduced 'Pills' into his set, maybe it was because of The New York Dolls!"

One sultry afternoon at the end of June, all of the Dolls went to Leber and Kreb's plush 65th Street office to sign on the dotted line. The boys in the band had taken no outside advice regarding their contracts, presuming that their management team were acting in their best interest. Instead of suggesting the band seek an independent attorney, Leber and Kreb's lawyer was present merely to oversee the signing. Arthur: "It meant that there was a conflict of interest and he also made us a counter offer. He told us not to sign with Leber and Krebs but to go with him instead." The sweet anaesthetic of chilled champagne was administered as the Dolls agreed to everything that was put before them, little realising that 'in perpetuity' meant forever. Sylvain: "They signed us all individually, plus as a band, plus our publishing, plus individual songwriting. They signed us everyway they could. They fucked us good and they didn't even give us a kiss." At 19, Johnny Thunders was the baby of the band, unaware that he should have had a parental co-signature. His contract could have been made void at any point up until his 21st birthday. Steve Leber and David Krebs were prepared to invest in the band but were particularly astute in their methods. Hit or miss, they wouldn't lose out. The balance of power in the managerial trinity didn't make the Mighty Thau look so mighty after all.

On signing, each Doll received a one-off $100 payment for clothes. A couple of amplifiers were purchased on their behalf, Peter Jordan was put on the payroll and the Dolls started to collect a weekly retainer of $75. In the meantime, the band's business guardians mapped out a career campaign. Steve Leber: "The plan was to establish their own identity. Marty, of course, had these crazy, off-the-wall ideas for them, because it was my money and his ideas. Quite frankly and honestly, we were willing to go the full limit. We did things that no one has ever done before in the record business. For instance, we found places where they could carve a niche in three or four different clubs in New York, like Max's Kansas City."

Sylvain and Billy were given temporary amnesty when the Dolls started playing upstairs in Max's, but had to leave as soon as the set was over. An article in *Rolling Stone* by Ed McCormack reported that the owner of Max's, Micky Ruskin, still had a low opinion of the band, regardless of the new custom they brought to the club, and was quoted as having said, "I guess they're a good draw, but I find them totally repulsive as individuals!"

The Dolls took the less snobbish Coventry in Queens by storm and established the club as a rock joint, then did much the same for Kenny's Castaways, a former singles bar on the Upper East Side of Manhattan. These tiny victories emboldened the management to send the band further afield. Peter Jordan: "They booked us at this club called Mr D's, a mafia dive in Long Island. Now, the further you go out of the city, the more provincial it becomes." The Dolls arrived at Mr D's with Jordan and Tony Machine (b. Krasinski), the youngest member of Leber and Kreb's staff, who had been appointed road manager for the evening. The radical change of scenery sent the band into culture shock. David: "Our managers were trying to see if we were viable outside of the East Village. The social situation there is unlike anywhere else, with its own rules or lack of them. So we went to this club and it was like something out of *American Graffiti*, with guys riding around in GTOs trying to attract chicks. It was like being on the moon to us."

The space cadets and crew made their way into the large barn-like club, complete with two bars. While a hard rock band finished their set with a Black Sabbath blow out, the Dolls were shown to their makeshift dressing room in the kitchen's service area. Once the conservative denim and moustache support act had left the stage, the Dolls revved into their first number. By the second song, the audience were divided. David: "All the chicks started moving to the front and all the guys went to the back. It all happened really fast, it must have been some primordial reaction to sexual confusion because the guys started beating the shit out of each other. The girls were looking at us in a trance while their boyfriends were killing each other. Then the bouncers opened the doors and started pushing people out of the club but some of the guys started jumping on the stage. I said, 'Fuck this' and went into the kitchen, grabbed a bottle and started sucking on it. Meanwhile, Billy comes out from behind the drums, he was a real rebel rouser, and he starts making a speech into the microphone, in his Colombian accent, about what assholes all the guys were. The owner of the club, this big muscular mob looking guy, grabs Billy by the ear and drags him off the stage and into the service area where we are. He sees that I've nicked a bottle from behind the bar, drops Billy and picks me up and throws me across the room like I was a pillow or something. I just lay where I'd hit the wall, like I was knocked out. The manager was in a rage because the whole night had gone to shit, so Tony Machine tried to calm him down, but the manager punched him in the nose. It was total bedlam. In the twenty minutes since we'd been on stage the club had gone from being packed to completely abandoned."

Outside, Peter Jordan kept his head down and packed up the equipment, claiming to be merely a hired hand for the night, getting on with his work. Peter: "Frankly, we could have all been killed. They could've broken our jaws easy." David and Billy saved the management from having to mete out any further punishment by finishing the job off between themselves in the parking lot. David: "We were ready to leave when Billy starts going at it, 'It's your fault!' and I'm like, 'No, it's yours!' until we're rolling around beating each other, you know till you get really red in the face and sweaty, it's kind of a good feeling. We were like two Puerto Rican Queens rolling round in the dirt. Then we went home. It was great."

Back in the Mercer Arts Center a different kind of drama was unfolding. David Bowie, already a big star in the UK, was desperate to repeat the process in America, not least to pay for his newly recruited and wildly profligate entourage. To this end, he began to associate with the cream of the NY Underground, put Wayne County on a MainMan retainer, and showed more than a passing interest in The New York Dolls. Bowie's presence in the Oscar Wilde Room, two nights in a row, was reported by Ed McCormack in *Rolling Stone*: 'Pale as an albino beneath his fiery cosmic crew cut, this elder statesman of the New Decadence is standing there in the shadows just off the dance floor in his white spacesuit, smiling broadly at the painted, talented young men on the bandstand. Still one cannot help but guess that somewhere in his enthusiasm a bitchy little doubt may be rearing its sequined sea horse head: so soon on the heels of his own success, could this be … the New Wave?' As a professional shape-shifter, Bowie started absorbing the Dolls. Sylvain: "He had all his bodyguards around him and he kept asking us questions. 'How did you get your hair like that? Where did you get your shoes?' I'm not saying that the Dolls turned him on to his feminine side, he already had that but we brought something out in him, his make-up got heavier and then he went out and got a pair of custom-made high backless mules, in the same style and from the same guy that we went to." Like an alien abduction, Billy Murcia and Cyrinda Foxe vanished into Angie and David Bowie's suite at The Plaza Hotel, only to re-emerge several long nights and short days later in a dishevelled state.

David Bowie's New York Dolls programme of assimilation came to a halt in the Bowery, where it all got a little too real for him. Luc Sante, in his history of New York, *Low Life*, described one of Manhattan's most infamous areas thus: "The Bowery has always possessed the greatest number of groggeries, flophouses, clip joints, brothels, fire sales, rigged auctions, pawnbrokers, dime museums, shooting galleries, dime-a-dance establishments, fortune telling salons, lottery agencies, thieves' markets and tattoo parlours, as well as theaters of the second, third, fifth and tenth rank. It is also a fact that the Bowery is the only major thoroughfare in New York never to have a single church built on it."

Through the stained-glass windows of his limousine, David Bowie eyed the raggedy forms of drunken bums in doorways as he went to meet the Dolls in their favourite watering hole, the Canal Street Center. Sylvain: "If you know Manhattan, this is where the jailhouse is. When they say in the movies 'Hey kid, we're taking you downtown' this is where you end up. We used to hang out on Canal Street, which goes all the way down to Third Avenue, which is the Bowery. It gets pretty funky down there and the bars are really cheap. It was Arthur's favourite place."

Being genial hosts, the Dolls thought Bowie might want to take an evening stroll. David Jo: "We were on Third Street and The Bowery, it was a pretty rough spot, and David Bowie does not want to be there. Then a big truck stopped at the light and the driver leans out and says to me 'Hey baby, I want to eat your cunt' and I'm going 'Well, you're just going to have to suck my dick, motherfucker.' Well, Bowie's knees are going, and he's like 'David, don't, please don't provoke him, David, please' and I'm yelling at the truck driver 'C'mon, get out of that truck you motherfucker!' " Bowie quickly bailed out of the band's orbit, returning to the safety of his fictional space station, where he wrote 'Watch That Man' apparently about

The New York Dolls. . . . 'Yeah, I was shaking like a leaf/For I couldn't undertand the conversation.'

The summer had succumbed to autumn but The New York Dolls still didn't have a record deal. They remained the toast of the Underground and had become the darlings of the press but no one was brave enough to sign them, fearing camp contamination. Marty Thau: "A&R people would come to see them but they couldn't see past the Dolls' exterior. They were such repressed times, people today wouldn't believe it. You couldn't even say 'Goddamn' on television. The issues of women's rights and gay and lesbian liberation had been put on the table, but they weren't put into practice. The music business perceived the Dolls as a bunch of degenerate queers. It was all down to homophobia."

The New York Dolls were the most talented pariahs in town. People from the record industry, even those that liked the band, would look but not dare to touch. Leee Black Childers: "The record companies were coming down but they weren't biting. Earl McGrath, who at that time was with Rolling Stones records, and had the best intentions in the world, would come to the Oscar Wilde Room, he'd be there dancing and then he'd dance away home and the poor little Dolls would be left going 'Where did Earl go?' The president of Atlantic Records, Ahmet Ertegun, came down, drank a little champagne, smoked a cigar, danced and had a great time, then, like Earl McGrath, he also went home."

Standing in the shadows of love, however, was Paul Nelson, a well respected rock journalist, who was now working as an A&R man at Mercury Records. Nelson had fallen head over heels for the band and began a one man campaign to get them signed. Paul Nelson: "As an A&R person, I thought my God, this is what it's like getting in on the ground floor of another Rolling Stones. I just loved the Dolls. I wanted to sign them and I didn't care what happened, I just wanted to be around the band." Because Nelson had been a journalist, and the Dolls were the Dolls, the rest of the team at Mercury were sceptical about his enthusiasm and assumed that Nelson was merely backing the latest critics' choice. Eventually, Nelson managed to persuade Charlie Fach, the head of A&R, to go and see the band with him. Paul Nelson: "The night Charlie Fach came to see them, they went on four hours late. Four minutes late would have been bad for Charlie. It seemed rather loveable at the time, people would be arriving for the second show and the first show hadn't gone ahead yet." Fach didn't find it quite as endearing and duly reported back to the Mercury team. The following week Lou Simon, from Mercury's head office in Chicago, also went to view the band, and this time they were only two hours late on stage. Simon loved them but Mercury's conservative decision makers were still undecided so, on October 8, Robin McBride, another of the company's A&R men, was dispatched to the Oscar Wilde Room. McBride had recently been responsible for signing a 13-piece horn act, who were so bad that people actually returned the demo tapes to the office. The Dolls were a mere hour late on for McBride, but Johnny in his platform basketball shoes managed to kick several holes in the stage while Arthur failed to notice that his bass had come unplugged for four songs. McBride was not impressed.

The managerial trinity scratched their heads: what next for their boys? Perhaps a European coup was the answer. Roy Hollingworth's ground breaking *Melody Maker* article had already given the band their UK introduction. Although just as repressed as the States, England had a different attitude towards drag and it was a smaller country to conquer. Steve Leber contacted a London promoter, Roy Fischer, who had worked with Alice Cooper and The Groundhogs. A deal was struck, Fischer would promote the Dolls if they would record a couple of songs for him. Leber and Fischer's fanciest move came when they got the Dolls a support slot to Rod Stewart and The Faces at the 8,000 seater Wembley Pool. Steve Leber: "The Dolls' time had not yet arrived here, so therefore we decided to go to England in order to get a record deal. We thought that the timing, their image and the excitement they could create would be incredible. I paid for the entire group to go."

The Dolls excitedly packed their vanity cases to breaking point with all their showgirls' outfits, chiffon blouses shoved next to sequinned hot pants, and all those wedged platform shoes that weighed a ton, but they didn't care. Even at the airport, when the immigration people were called, and Sylvain was held back until a later flight because he wasn't a US citizen, and Billy's papers were a mess, and Johnny lost his ID, nothing was going to bring them down 'cos they were hauling their boogie to London.

4
Death Trip

A horse and cart awaited The New York Dolls at Heathrow. The novelty transport was arranged as a publicity stunt by Roy Fischer and Escape Studios, but as the Dolls took their places in the back of the hay-filled cart, it looked more like a tumbrel *en route* to the guillotine. Eventually they switched to a car and were driven to Escape Studios in Kent.

The studio was located in a converted oast house, complete with accommodation, and over a couple of heavy drinking days The Dolls again recorded versions of 'Personality Crisis', 'Looking For A Kiss' and 'Bad Girl'. The old Actress number 'That's Poison', which had been revamped and rewritten as 'Subway Train', was also laid down. A high speed melodrama, David Johansen is convincing as the estranged lover boy ... 'See a train coming down a lonely track/Well I'm hoping it's going to bring my baby back'. The lyrics tail off into the American folk standard 'Dinah's In The Kitchen', an example of Johansen's eclectic cut, paste and collage writing technique in which references to anything from movie stars to television shows and favourite groups like The Shangri-Las might be found. The Escape sessions show a marked progression from the earlier Blue Rock recordings; the band are tighter and have a better relationship with their chosen instruments, despite the copious amounts of liquor they'd consumed.

Steve Leber checked into The Dorchester, while Marty Thau and the Dolls had reservations at The Whitehouse, by all accounts a fairly dismal hotel in South Kensington. After completing their recording obligations to Fischer, the band did a one-off show at The Speakeasy, then London's hippest hot spot. Peter Jordan: "It wasn't very well set up, it had a really crampy PA. The thinking behind it was that we should play the most popular club in London. What ... in front of every jaded son of a bitch who works in the English rock press, so they can all laugh at us. I saw John Entwistle there and I slapped him on the back, I loved The Who, the whole band did, and he nearly punched me!" On October 26, the Dolls somewhat inappropriately supported The Groundhogs, a trio led by the accomplished blues guitarist Tony McPhee, at the Alhambra Rock in Birmingham. Before the show the band were presented with a couple of crates of Newcastle Brown ale, which Murcia violently regurgitated during their set.

Like so many other bands of the time, The New York Dolls ran on a diet of booze and chemicals. Unlike their peers, however, the Dolls never knew how or when to stop. All the rock'n'roll compulsions were getting to Billy Murcia, but because the whole band was riding on a roller coaster, no one really noticed that he was ailing more than the others. That cute looking girl, Marilyn, and her friend that he'd met at The Speakeasy, had sorted him out with some mandies. He guessed they were kind of like downers, 'ludes or tuinol or valium or something. Whatever, they helped you sleep when your head was too full of rock'n'roll glory to slow down.

On Sunday, October 29, The New York Dolls played the biggest gig of their entire career at The Wembley Festival of Music, sandwiched between The Pink Fairies and the head-liners, Rod Stewart and The Faces. The charity event, which lasted for the whole weekend, was organised by The Stars Organisation For Spastics. Sylvain: "Boy, were we ever perfect for that. There couldn't have been more spastic rock'n'rollers in the world." Suddenly the Dolls were going to have to turn on an audience of 8,000 in what was then known as the Wembley Empire Pool. The maximum capacity they'd ever played to before had been little more than 200. At sound check, they clustered together in their usual formation, unsure as to how they were going to work the massive stage.

They were daunted but attitude prevailed.

Sylvain: "It was huge, all we were used to was the Mercer Arts Center and if any of the other guys have ever said they weren't scared, it's not true. We were such nice boys for that gig, we did everything we were supposed to do, we arrived at the sound check on time and when some member of royalty came into the dressing room and gave us a bottle of champagne, we stood up and bowed like we were told to, no problem baby!" As the patron of The Spastics Society, the Duchess Of Kent went meeting and greeting all the bands on the bill. Had she been a lesser dame, the Dolls might have tried to relieve her of her tiara, which no doubt would have ended up crowning David Johansen, who's self-importance had of late become royally inflated.

After an introduction by compere Emperor Rosko, the Dolls attempted to warm up the largely hostile Wembley crowd. Mark Plummer reviewed their set for *Melody Maker*: "The New York Dolls played what was possibly one of the worst sets I've seen. Their glamour bit brought wolf whistles and shouts to go before a note had been played, and by the time a string had broken on Johnny Thunders' Plexiglas guitar they had lost what audience sympathy they had. Musically their set was dire and failed to gel, their two guitarists play all the old tired licks. And who really wants to know about 'Pill City'? Wembley didn't for sure." One young thug with aspirations to be in a band, who had broken in through the back of the venue in order to see The Faces and the Dolls, vehemently disagreed with Mark Plummer's critical hammering. Future Sex Pistol Steve Jones: "The Dolls played rock'n'roll music how I liked to hear it, kinda sloppy. I was a real big fan of The Faces but they were a bit more controlled, more like good time music but the Dolls were seriously crazy and I'd never seen anything like that. I don't think anyone had. The audience hated them and started slinging shit at them but they kept on playing. They were great, wild."

After the show Kit Lambert, The Who's manager and the

boss of Track Records, took the Dolls plus Steve Leber and Marty Thau out to dinner. Lambert was seriously courting the band, and had booked an expensive restaurant for their use only. Born into a gilded but tragic family, Lambert was one of rock'n'roll's great profligate aristocrats, a fop with a taste for "boys in black leather raincoats and eyes like swimming pools" as he admitted in an interview shortly before his death in 1981. Although Lambert consumed massive quantities of drink and drugs, he still had plenty of clout and money to offer the Dolls and he organised a lively social calendar for them. Peter Jordan: "We went to a Guy Fawkes party at Kit Lambert's town house. It was really beautiful but it was empty 'cos he'd only just moved in. At the top of the stairs, there was a closet with a real skeleton in it, and a coffin. Speedy Keene was being the DJ and I remember Keith Moon saying that he'd put a bomb in the garden."

Although The New York Dolls didn't yet know it, they had reached their summit. They hadn't peaked musically but in London they were a hair's breadth away from real stardom. Though it never truly would be again, at this brief moment everything they had ever wanted was within their grasp. Arthur Kane: "Six months earlier we'd been standing in the street, looking at boots in a shop window, thinking 'Gee, I wish I could afford to buy those' and six months later we're partying with The Who. We were fans of theirs but now we're The New York Dolls and we've got instant fame."

Mick Jagger flew in to London from Ireland specifically to see the Dolls when they played at the Imperial College, sharing a bill with Status Quo and Capability Brown. The Dolls were, in effect, auditioning for Rolling Stone Records and even though Jagger was friendly enough to the band, he later quipped in print: "Yeah, I've seen The New York Dolls. We were almost going to sign 'em up at one point. I went down to the Imperial College gig and – uh, their lead singer – I saw 'er and I just didn't think much of it at all." Mick Taylor backed Jagger's opinion when he told the press: "(The Dolls) were the worst high school band I ever saw", leaving Johansen to retort: "No, we're the best high school band you ever saw! The kids will love us!"

Richard Branson, who had recently launched Virgin Records, sent a hand-written introductory note to Steve Leber by courier to The Dorchester. Marty Thau: "He had a houseboat on the Thames, so we shot across town in a car and got on to this hippy houseboat. In the back of it was this young guy with long hair, a fuzzy face and a flowery Nehru shirt on. He said, 'I've heard such great things about the Dolls, I'd like to sign them to Virgin and I'd be willing to offer you $5,000.' We said, 'Well, we don't think there is much of a conversation here because we're interested in £350,000. Thank you Richard, it was nice meeting you.'" Tony Stratton-Smith, owner of Charisma Records, was particularly keen to sign the Dolls and made several journeys to Steve Leber's hotel suite, but Leber decided Charisma was unsuitable. Everything was going to plan and although Leber and Thau wanted to wait before making a final decision, as other offers were coming in, Track Records was the favoured contender.

Kit Lambert continued to woo the Dolls, introducing them to high and low society. Johnny's revealing skin-tight red leather suit, a Barbara Troiani creation, made him rather popular among some of Lambert's pals but certain tensions in the Dolls' ranks were upsetting their London honeymoon. Sylvain: "This Sir, Lord 'Wanna-suck-your-cock . . . whatever', sends his Rolls round to the hotel to pick us all up. David interpreted that the car was being sent just for him. So, like a Keystone cartoon we all piled in without David, and off we go. Meanwhile, we're at the party and in marches David Johansen, really pissed off. He goes 'You fucking guys, you took the fucking car, you didn't even wait for me, who the fuck do you think you are?' He comes out with all this crap over the stupid car, and how he'd had to take a cab. Then he starts screaming at Billy 'cos he was the one that told the driver to go. He always screamed at Billy more than the rest of us. He was kind of mean like that." After Johansen's irate entrance, the party got into full swing, Liberace played the piano and Syl got to meet his hero, the actor Sal Mineo.

The Dolls were like children in a garden of delightful nights but one of them was literally being spoiled to death. Sylvain: "We were going to all these parties and, of course, there would be drugs going round. Being the darlings of the town isn't the safest or most sensible position to be in, especially in those days when you were up for trying anything."

On November 4, The New York Dolls opened for Argent at the Mile End Sundown in East London before making the long journey to Liverpool where they had a support slot to Lou Reed at The Stadium. The Dolls got as far as the Stadium's dressing room when Reed sent in one of his flunkies with a terse message to the effect that Lou wouldn't set foot on the stage if the Dolls went on. Marty Thau: "I don't know what Lou Reed's problem was. Ten minutes before they were supposed to play, they were told that he wasn't going to do the show if they went on. It was really cruel and mean. I couldn't possibly figure out why he did that, the reason had to be some nasty little insecurity." Still smarting from the rejection, The Dolls went out for dinner at The New York Steakhouse in Liverpool's town centre. Sylvain: "Mr Lou Reed took away our best moment there. As far as I'm concerned he was a fucking scumbag, because it really broke Billy and those were his last days."

The next date on The Dolls' itinerary was on November 9 at Manchester's Hardrock, with Roxy Music. With a couple of days to spare the band hung out in London. Arthur and Peter Jordan were looking to score some decent pot, Johnny and Janis went shopping, David kept trying to call Cyrinda but she was busy with David Bowie in California, where they were shooting a mini-movie to coincide with the release of 'Jean Jeanie'. Sylvain was canoodling with an heiress called Valerie and Billy was spending time with Speakeasy Marilyn and her girlfriend. Sylvain: "One morning I saw Billy walking round the lobby. We started chatting and he said, 'Sylvain, I almost died last night.' I said, 'What do you mean, you almost died? What happened?' 'I was with those girls and I've been taking a lot of MXs (Mandrax a.k.a. Mandies).' He told me he'd been very smart, 'cos all he'd taken was half of what he'd been given, then he went inside his shirt pocket to show me the other 10 or 15 half tabs he had left. He had a weak stomach and drinking never agreed with him so I said, 'C'mon man, what's with all this stuff?' It really never hit me at the time, but what I should have done was sat him down and told him to stop with it."

The following day, the whole band regrouped for a meal in the hotel restaurant. Sylvain: "Johansen was sitting there and he started in on Billy. Now Billy had the two girls sitting with him and Johansen started humiliating him in front of them, it was really bad and it was uncalled for. He just wanted to pull this stupid power crap . . . 'Listen, you fuck up one more time and you're out. I don't give a shit who the fuck you are, what the hell are you doing, this is my band, I'm the singer, this is my career dahdahdahdah.' He bawled Billy out so fucking bad, that was the worse one he ever gave him. Of course, Billy walked out, he was really mad, in tears. It was so horrible and Johansen kept right on going. We all left the table. Then a couple of hours later we get the crazy phone call, that something had happened to Billy."

Billy's tearful departure from the restaurant was the last time any of the band saw him alive. Exactly what happened to Murcia between the hours of 8 and 11pm on Tuesday, November 7, has never been truly established. Conflicting accounts, speculation turned to fact by the passage of time and the vague possibility of a hasty cover-up designed to protect someone outside of the band who was present when their drummer was dying, makes ascertaining the absolute truth almost impossible. Marty Thau has always maintained that Billy met his fate because of a crossed phone wire coincidence. Thau: "I got a phone call from Billy Murcia asking me if I could give him £5 so I said sure. He told me that he had gotten a phone call from these people who were having a party and that they were looking for someone. They thought Billy was who they were looking for. In conversation, he mentioned to them that he was in a group called The New York Dolls. The people on the line got very excited and invited him to their party at such and such an address. He didn't have any plans, so he accepted. He came down to my room and picked up the extra couple of bucks. We had a limo downstairs so I told him he could use that, then to send the driver back because Steve Leber and I had to see some people."

According to a story in the *Kensington News and Post*, headlined 'Pop Group Drowning Tragedy' written by a journalist who attended the inquest at the Westminster Coroner's Court on November 24, evidence given by Billy's London girl, Marilyn Woolhead, contradicts Thau's recollections. Although she was described as a model in the *Kensington News*, Arthur Kane maintained that Woolhead was an international call girl with Mafia connections. In her statement to the coroner, Woolhead said that Billy called her about 8pm, and she invited him over to her flat in Brompton Lodge on the Cromwell Road. He arrived between half an hour and an hour later, in an okay condition. "He didn't seem absolutely sober, but he didn't seem that drunk," she said. With Woolhead were two of her friends, James Owen, an actor, and Malcolm Raines, a fashion designer, who both lived in Chelsea. Raines left the flat while James Owen, Billy and Marilyn shared a bottle of champagne between them. When Malcolm Raines returned, he found Billy lying on the bed, incoherent.

Marilyn Woolhead then detailed the trio's resuscitation attempts: "We tried to get him to move over and he didn't, so we tried to wake him up. I went and made some black coffee and the others put him in the bath." Murcia was carried down the hall and lowered into an icy bath by the two men. "When I've been drunk, it's been done to me before," James Owen told the coroner. Owen and Raines denied that they let Billy's head tilt back into the water. They kept him upright so that they could give him black coffee, while managing to hold ice against the back of his neck. After their misguided efforts at first aid failed, Marilyn slapped Billy around, still hoping to bring him out of it. Owen and Raines then tried to get him to walk down the hall, supported between them, but noted that the wet rag Doll's feet were dragging. Finally Marilyn Woolhead called for an ambulance. Back in the bedroom, they attempted to dress Murcia, but why, in an emergency situation, would anyone lose precious moments by unnecessarily stripping someone off in the first place? James Owen employed a little more of his medical know-how: "I felt for his heart beat and it felt to me as if it was beating."

The Coroner, Gavin Thurston, who in 1970 presided over the inquest of Jimi Hendrix, recorded a verdict of accidental death. "By far the best thing to have done would have been to get an ambulance straight away and certainly not put a person in a bath of water," he said.

It may have been an oversight but nowhere in the fairly comprehensive *Kensington News* inquest coverage is any mention made of the methaqualone content ingested by Murcia and recorded by the Coroner. The cause of death given on the certificate is . . . "drowning in a domestic bath while under the influence of alcohol and methaqualone". Usually known as mandrax, a form of barbiturate, methaqualone can be lethal when taken with alcohol, which is why they were eased off the market. As Murcia still had some life left in him, no matter how incoherent he appeared to be when the trio first tried to revive him, with proper care he would have probably come around, but in the Seventies drug education was practically unheard of and second-hand drug folklore was usually employed.

Further questions would forever hang over the awful chain of events. Marty Thau recalls that he and Steve Leber were on the verge of signing the Dolls to Track Records for £100,000 at the apartment of Kit Lambert's friend, fellow impressario

Tony Secunda. Secunda, Lambert and his business partner Chris Stamp, were all present when the phone rang and someone whose identity has never been revealed asked for Marty and told him that Billy was dead. How did the anonymous caller know where to find Thau? The limousine driver who had dropped Billy off at Brompton Lodge had returned to the hotel to chauffeur Marty and Steve Leber to their appointment with Lambert. Thau: "I put down the phone and walked out of the meeting. I was so shocked. I hailed a cab and went over to the address the caller had given. There were four or five people up in this apartment building and Billy was propped up on the floor in a sitting position, against the bed, dead. Scotland Yard were there, I identified his body and answered a few questions. Then the Dolls pulled up in a couple of cars."

Steve Leber remembered being at The Dorchester and getting a call from someone at Scotland Yard who asked if he knew a Billy Murcia, then the news was broken to him. Leber dashed over to the Dolls' hotel, filled them in on what little he knew and told them to immediately ditch any drugs in their possession. Peter Jordan: "I was with Arthur, sitting in the hotel room and we were pretty happy 'cos we'd finally gotten some pot. It was from Africa and it had been pressed into a brick and was as hard as a fucking rock. We were just about to skin up when either Syl or Johnny came in and told us that Billy was dead. It was a huge shock. I mean everyone had been out nearly every night of the week partying, but to die here in London, the most civilised capital of the western world ... how could he have managed to go out and die? I guess no one thought they could die. The pot went right out the window. We were expecting the door to fly open and to be dragged off to the Old Bailey but we didn't get interviewed by the police."

The 'Do Not Disturb' sign was still up on Sylvain's door when he was informed of his best friend's passing. After the unpleasant scene at dinner, Syl had gone up to his room and crashed out for a couple of hours but his dreams had been kind of strange. Later, they would haunt him. Sylvain: "At the particular moment when Billy was in trouble, the people that loved him weren't even thinking about him and he slipped through the cracks. I was dreaming right before we got the phone call and I'll always remember this because I felt very guilty. I always thought I had something to do with his death because he kind of came to me in my dream and said, 'I've got to go now' and I dreamed back to him, 'Well, if you've got to go now, don't worry, go'. For years I carried around this guilt because I said he could go. The mind has ways of playing tricks on you. Johnny always felt a lot of guilt, too."

Johnny Thunders arrived at Brompton Lodge minutes before Sylvain. "I got out of the cab and Johnny looked at me and said 'Syl, don't even go upstairs, he's dead already' and that was it, I started screaming."

Thau and Leber sent the stricken band members back to the hotel, while they stayed on helping Scotland Yard with their inquiries. Marty remembers watching the police take the details of fifty or so young people who had showed up for a party at Marilyn Woolhead's apartment, some of whom had apparently been present during Billy's final moments. As the crowd dispersed, illuminated by the flashing lights of the emergency services, Thau tried to get more details but all he came up with was some rumours about morphine in Brompton Lodge. Aside from Marilyn Woolhead, James Owen and Malcolm Raines, no other public testimony has ever been offered. Somehow, fifty potential witnesses vanished without trace. Later in the mid-Seventies, however, a series of drug busts in and around Chelsea and Kensington netted many children of aristocrats and politicians.

Tony Secunda had followed Thau to Brompton Lodge out of shock and concern, but the ramification's of Murcia's demise were obvious. Marty Thau: "All bets were off at that point. What record company was going to invest one penny in a group if they didn't even know they were going to carry on? Would they be worse or what? How long would it take them to break in a new drummer and would he be the right or wrong choice for the band?" Meanwhile, Sylvain's New York girl-friend Elda Gentile had phoned the hotel to speak to him. Elda: "I just wanted to know how he was doing. I got him on the line and I couldn't comprehend anything that he said, he was hysterical, except for the words 'Billy is dead'." Sylvain then made the dreaded call to Billy's sister Heidi in New York. She was sharing Billy and Johnny's 14th Street apartment, which they'd moved into after losing the Chrystie Street loft.

Reports about Murcia's death in the music press were minimal. Notification was given that The New York Dolls would no longer be supporting Roxy Music in Manchester and that the band had left the country following their drummer's tragic demise. The news blackout was engineered by a concerned Thau. "I made up my mind that the thing to do was to send the Dolls back to New York on the first plane in the morning because I suspected that this could grow into a big rock'n'roll scandal. It was certain to be ammunition for *Melody Maker* and *NME* and I wanted to spare the band and the Murcia family more than anyone, the pain and the anguish. Their son was dead and he died under such a grey cloud, or at least that would be the way it would be manipulated and portrayed." Unfortunately because of the lack of any detailed communications and the band's reputation for being a sluttish scourge on society, it was presumed that Murcia had overdosed. From here on in, The New York Dolls, already tagged as transvestite fags by the music industry, would also be labelled as drug addicts.

Marty Thau and Steve Leber stayed on in London for a couple of extra days, helping the police with their paperwork, while the Dolls went home. Sylvain: "We're on the plane the next day. The stewardess comes up to us and says, 'How come you're all crying?' I said, 'We're in a band. Yesterday there was five, now there's only four.' " On arrival in New York, they all went to the 14th Street apartment until late in the evening. Round 11pm, Sylvain went over to Elda's to collect some of his belongings. Elda: "He was a mess. He was still in the same clothes he'd been wearing in England. Somehow his jeans had split down the sides but he was so out of it, he had no idea what he looked like. He said: 'Elda, I have to stay with Johnny.' He was so devastated. After that, I'd still see him but he wasn't the same. Arthur, he always used to drink and be out of it but now he seemed depressed and Johnny, well you know what happened to Johnny with dope."

Sylvain moved into his best friend's room, which was still in the same mess that Billy had left behind a lifetime ago when he'd been packing for the English trip. Sylvain: "It was weird living in Billy's room. He was my best friend. He was like my little brother. We'd done everything together from being little immigrants who came into the country, our struggles with the clothing thing and going through the Sixties. We had such a gas together. I still miss him."

Murcia's body was returned to his family in a sealed metal container almost a month after his death. The delay was caused by the inquest and the fact that Billy's passport was deemed to be illegal by the British authorities. Steve Leber's friend, Dick Asher, then president of CBS, Columbia Records' London company, sorted out the unfortunate situation. One cold afternoon in early December, a bedraggled bunch of mourners gathered together in a cemetery in Westchester County to say a final goodbye to Billy Murcia.

In the immediate aftermath, the Dolls were too shattered to make any decisions. David Johansen: "When we came back I didn't have a clue about what we were going to do. It wasn't like what are we going to do? It was, well we aren't going to do anything. We were like brothers in a way, it was pretty heavy." While the band were in retreat, a ripple of public sympathy turned into a wave. Marty Thau fielded calls from magazines around the world and David Bowie offered his condolences. The *Village Voice* did a major piece lambasting those who accidentally colluded in Murcia's death. Thau: "The article only added to the interest. When a death occurs in a rock'n'roll band it adds sinister proportions. The Dolls were beginning to receive adulation on a grander scale than just their few compadres in the East Village. Then I heard from the band, they wanted to carry on and were auditioning for a drummer."

Ironically, Murcia's demise got the Dolls' the attention they'd been hoping for but it was at the kind of wretched price the devil favours. Leee Black Childers: "Instead of sobering them up it made them crazier. It affected Johnny a whole lot. He'd had a real innocence about him but when Billy died he started to change his attitude and maybe it triggered his plunge into self-destruction. The death of Billy Murcia was the death of the Dolls, as we had loved them."

5

Notorious

From the moment that Jerry Nolan first saw Johnny Thunders hanging out by the fountain in Central Park, all those years ago, he knew that someday they'd be in a band together. Jerry: "The first time I met Johnny, I said, 'Do you play?' He said, 'Yeah, I play bass.' I said, 'We're gonna be in a band together.' I felt it and I knew it." Now destiny had dealt him the card. Before the auditions at the Charles Lane studio had even begun, Nolan was sure that he was the main contender. Sylvain: "We always knew that Jerry was going to be our drummer, not because we loved him or that he was so groovy, but because we all played in the same kind of bands and performed in the same houses."

The only other drummer that came close to being competition for Nolan was Marc Bell, who would eventually join The Ramones. Billy Murcia had respected Nolan's skills and on occasion even borrowed his kit. Jerry Nolan was ambitious, he'd played on the outskirts of success for too long. Originally from Brooklyn, Nolan became a mobile army brat when his mother remarried a soldier. Jerry: "He was stationed in Hawaii so we moved there for about three years then he got stationed in Oklahoma and we went there for another three years. Then we went back to New York."

Along the way, Jerry learned to play drums. A young black soldier on the army base in Hawaii gave Nolan his first lesson, then when the family settled in Oklahoma, Jerry joined the high school band where he befriended saxophonist Buddy Bowser. At 14, he started drumming in strip joints. Nolan lived the kind of life much loved by *vérité* movie makers: a little Chet

Baker and a lot of rock'n'roll. In New York he would sleep on bar tops after gigs because he couldn't afford to stay in a hotel. He'd seen Elvis and Eddie Cochran, could make a zip gun out of a car aerial and left his Brooklyn Street gang to play rock'n'roll.

Prior to joining The New York Dolls, Nolan played wherever he could. Jerry: "Before I was in the Dolls, I used to have to settle for playing with lots of different type bands. I auditioned for Suzi Quatro and everything worked out well, so I drove back to Detroit with them. I lived with them all summer, did a few gigs but it ended up that Suzi got an offer from an English guy and you know what happened to her career after that. I went back to New York where I was playing with all kinds of people. I even played with an old Italian guy in bars all over Queens. Then I started playing with Wayne County, that was when the Dolls were formed. I started to get to know the boys, especially Billy."

He lit a cigarette, flexed his powerful hands and sat down behind the drums at Charles Lane studio. He never missed a beat, so sure was he of his own prowess. Jerry would later tell the *Village Voice*: "I played the whole set in the audition like I had been playing with them for ten years. I added a little bit more. Each song I would change just a little bit. I didn't want to overdo it, because they would get lost. They weren't very professional yet. I gave them just enough so they'd notice that there could be more done with the song than they had been doing with it. I was so on it was pathetic. I remember Arthur walked over to me after we played 'Personality Crisis'. He said, 'Wow, I've never played that song so fast in my life.'"

After the audition Jerry and the band went to Max's. In the backroom they toasted their new drummer. A huge grin lit up his normally immobile features. Gail Higgins Smith: "I remember Jerry running up to me saying, 'Can you believe it, I'm going to be a Doll!' He was so excited. Jerry and I started going out for a while then, but he was already taking downs, so it was a short-lived romance." The next morning Johnny met

Jerry on 14th Street and took him up to the apartment he shared with Syl to present him with his Dolly trousseau.

Unlike Billy, Syl and Johnny who were made for the role, Jerry Nolan wasn't a natural born Doll. He was more a dandified street tough. Johansen was a good actress, Kane was shameless in his tutus but Nolan had to learn and, despite his love of street style, he occasionally looked a little awkward in his Dolly drag. Sylvain: "We took Jerry around, got him Dolled up, went to the New York branch of the Chelsea Cobbler with him so he could get some boots. He did his best but he went a little bit like David, and played it like a gay guy, which he wasn't."

Suitably attired, Nolan was introduced to the management team. In spite of the disastrous recent events, there was still optimism in the Dolls' camp. Marty Thau: "We went to this restaurant in Little Italy to celebrate the newest member in the group. It was nice between all of us. We were still good friends, we admired each other and we had great hopes. All of us believed, without any reservation, that The New York Dolls were going to be one of the biggest groups in the world. I was praying that The Rolling Stones would break up because of all the comparisons that were being made between the Dolls and the Stones and the reality that David even looked a little like Mick Jagger. People started asking, 'Are the Dolls the American Stones or some kind of impersonation?' and I would say, 'No, not at all' but that did become a superficial evaluation of who and what the Dolls were." More worldly than the rest of his new cohorts, Nolan made sure he got the most out of signing with the managers and promptly acquired three drumkits, two sets of Slingerland, one green and one white, together with a divine pink customised Ludwig. He also insisted upon a $600 couch, and got it.

On December 19, 1972, Jerry Nolan made his début with the Dolls. This time the band were booked into one of the largest rooms in the Mercer Arts Center. The Sean O' Casey Theater had tiered seating that surrounded a central performance platform and could hold an audience of 450. With all the renewed interest in the Dolls, Steve Leber decided to turn Jerry's first show with the band into a record industry convention and he invited all the top brass in town. By their very nature, the Dolls were an unpredictable band and without their own crowd to up the adrenalin level, they floundered. Sylvain: "The Dolls, even with Jerry Nolan, had their good nights and their bad nights. It was art and way before the time of stage tuners. We used to tune up to David's harmonica, it'd take us an hour. A lot of times we sucked, we didn't know how to play but we were so inventive. We were cute, we moved pretty good and it was sexy but that night we blew it fucking big. Every major record company passed on us."

It wasn't just an off night that alienated the music business. One label reported back to Thau that Johansen was great but the band sucked, while another thought the band were great and Johansen sucked. However, there was another altogether more insidious reason why The New York Dolls were failing to get a record deal and it had nothing to do with matters of personal taste or the band's competence or even lack of it. Marty Thau: "There were all these nasty little whispers about the group. The moralists in the industry were saying, 'Don't sign them because they're bad for the youth of America, keep them out.' There was someone in particular, someone who had and still has a lot of power, which is why I can't tell you his name, that had a word with me about the Dolls. They touched a nerve with him and he wanted to keep them out of the industry. The moralist that he was. He has so many nasty skeletons in his own closet. He's so hypocritical, it's nauseating." Thau, who since the collapse of the band has been all but ostracised by the mainstream music business, cannot reveal the main perpetrator behind the 'Moral' campaign against The New York Dolls for fear of legal reprisals.

Paul Nelson, however, was still beseeching Mercury Records to take the Dolls, so much so that he was willing to put his own career on the line for them. Irwin Steinberg, the president of Mercury, who in his spare time liked to design golf clubs, had been at the Wembley Pool gig primarily to see Rod Stewart, but he also caught the Dolls' set. Nelson: "When Irwin came back from London we had an A&R meeting in Chicago and he told me that if I ever brought up The New York Dolls again, I would be fired on the spot. He said they were the worst bunch of amateurs he had ever seen in his life. Immediately after he said all that, I said 'I wish you'd reconsider' and he walked away from me."

On January 30, 1973, Mike Gormley, the head of publicity at Mercury Records, flew in from Chicago to see the Dolls play Kenny's Castaways. Gormley immediately issued a memo to all departments at Mercury strongly recommending that the company sign The New York Dolls at once. Paul Nelson then laid in wait for Irwin Steinberg. Nelson: "I decided to try this one final pitch. If I was going to get fired, I didn't want it to be in the office. Steinberg had come in from Chicago and I found out where he was staying. I sat up all night in the hotel lobby waiting, because I knew he'd come down for breakfast. He did a double take when he saw me sitting there at 6.30 in the morning. He said, 'What are you doing here?' I told him I wanted to speak to him about something really important and I didn't want to do it in the office. I said, 'You've really got to reconsider this Dolls thing. Even if you don't like them, they are a viable band that people want to see. They are really good, look at all these press clippings, and I didn't write any of them.' After that things started happening fairly quickly. I don't know if it would have worked without Mike Gormley's input and the accumulation of press."

With an impending deal with Mercury on the cards, it was decided to expand the road crew. Max Blatt came in as a drum roadie and Keeth Paul took over the sound duties, while Desmond Sullivan helped lighten Peter Jordan's work load. Only the Dolls, at this stage of the game, could have employed a valet. Christian Rodriguez, a.k.a. Frenchy, had been a sergeant in Vietnam who had worked as a colour co-ordinator with Sylvain when Truth & Soul was in operation. He was drafted into the Dolls' crew to take care of their wardrobe and any other loose ends, which was an infinitesimal task. Peter Jordan: "Frenchy worked in this clothing store, he had great taste and would give us stuff off the rack, fast. He was a very good-looking guy, we called him Frenchy because he would pick up girls by pretending he was French, in fact he was Spanish. He was a very nice guy and he was hired to be in charge of the wardrobe which was pretty extensive. He would also be in charge of who got through the door to see the band. I would be too busy with everything else to deal with sixty Colombians waiting outside the dressing room who all claimed to know Syl. Frenchy was a slight-looking guy but he could kick some ass. He was smart and he would keep an eye on our own troublemakers. At that point, we had one troublemaker and that was Mr Genzale. He'd aggravate people, you'd go someplace and he'd tell someone to go fuck themselves and the next minute they'd be trying to kill you. Eventually Frenchy graduated from wardrobe to babysitting Johnny."

On February 11, the Dolls headlined 'An Endless Valentine's Day All-Night Party' at the Mercer Arts Center with Queen Elizabeth featuring Wayne County, Suicide, and Eric Emerson and The Magic Tramps as the main support acts. Miles reviewed the event for the English music press. So taken was he with the entire spectacle that even the fans came under the spotlight. "The audience could well have been in the group, a woman with black lipstick looked dead, very weird scene, many men wore full drag, a man near me with a full beard also disported a floor-length red ball gown and ethereal smile. Some couples wore unisex make-up and were hard to distinguish from each other in the welter of day-glo, lurex, tinsel, glitter dust on flesh, and clothes, studs, satin, silk and leather, lurid reds, pink angora tops, green boas, totally transparent blouses and of course everyone had gained at least three inches in their multi-coloured platforms. The total effect was quite sinister after London which still tends more towards the warmth and friendliness of lace and velvet, whereas NY is cold and distant in silk and satin, the faces remote in dead white make-up like wandering ghosts of a lost humanity." Next Miles tackled the Dolls and forever banished the idea that being in a band was strictly a hetero male-only activity. "OK here come The NY Dolls. The lead singer looks like Jagger, same big mouth and everything. The lead guitarist looks a bit like Keith. They have modelled themselves on the Stones, a terrible alter-ego Rolling Stones, come to haunt Mick'n'Keith and the boys with a direct expression of all that camping on stage. A hard rock, camp prissy 100% homosexual group in black tights posturing and imitating all of Mick's stage gestures and leaps. It's terrific!"

What straight males often fail to understand is that young girls love pretty boys. Teenage icons are seldom muscle men. *16* magazine, the pin-up bible that at the time featured spreads of Donny Osmond and David Cassidy and had once given the world those smouldering shots of Jim Morrison topless in a fur coat, also included The New York Dolls in their photographic pantheon of desirable pop stars. The Dolls presented a wilder notion of the teen tease that was at best confusing and at worst revolting to certain sectors of the population.

Photographer Bob Gruen understood the Dolls' appeal. Gruen: "You have to realise that things were different back then. The Dolls were quite shocking and some people got frightened when they saw guys wearing women's clothes in public. Until very recently it had been illegal for men to wear women's clothing in public. It wasn't just different or odd, it was illegal and immoral and nobody cared if you beat up a fag. That's what the Stonewall riots (the birth of the Gay Libera-tion movement in 1969) were all about. By law, a man could not impersonate a woman. If he even put on lipstick, he was subject to arrest and that still applied in many states up until 1991. Even today, people are not allowed to have same sex relationships in Alabama and that includes in the privacy of their own home. The interesting thing about the Dolls was although they were frightening in the sense of wearing women's clothes, they didn't dress as women. They weren't transvestites, they didn't wear wigs or push-up bras. They wore bright, tight, see-through clothing, you didn't see breasts, what you saw was a really well defined dick. The Dolls let it all hang out and painted it up and put on platform shoes so it was pretty much in your face and they were getting all the pretty girls. People were saying they were faggots but the girls knew they weren't. The Dolls were attracting really desirable, eligible women. I was impressed."

Gruen, now one of the most in-demand rock photographers in the world, was already making a name for himself when he came upon the Dolls. He'd worked with John Lennon and Yoko Ono and was Ike and Tina Turner's tour photographer. He'd also begun video taping acts on a cumbersome reel-to-reel video machine. Gruen's pioneering attempts at video making were not meant for commercial use, rather they gave the artists a chance to see themselves in action. Tina Turner used Bob's b&w footage to check that The Ikettes were doing the right moves and grooves behind her during their shows. Even though Gruen hadn't yet been commissioned to work with the Dolls, he started taking pictures of them because they were such a visual treat. He also began filming them. Bob Gruen: "I taped the Dolls at Kenny's Castaways but I still hadn't really talked to David yet, apart from a backstage hello and the odd photo. Then I went to Max's one night and David was at the bar and I stopped to tell him that I had this tape. We really hit it off. David was entertaining and clever and funny. He and Cyrinda came over to see the video and eventually so did the whole band, and they all liked it. I started showing some of the tapes on early morning cable TV on the public access station. I started documenting more and more of the Dolls, I'd just leave the tape running. I was doing this on my own money but I had other paying jobs going on with Alice Cooper, Suzi Quatro and Kiss."

The rise of The New York Dolls spawned dozens of local bands. Elda Gentile got The Stilettos together with former Max's waitress, Debbie Harry, and Rick Rivets started gigging with The Brats, while a rash of Dolls copyists like Teenage Lust and The Harlots of 42nd Street threw themselves on the bandwagon and fell belly-up. Aside from Aerosmith, the most significant group of that time to be influenced by The New York Dolls was Kiss. Sure, Kiss wore make-up but by painting their faces like comic-book characters or goofy animals, they defused any sexual threat. Their songs were direct, clap along rock'n'roll and they established themselves at all the venues the Dolls had put on the map, from The Diplomat Hotel to the Coventry in Queens. Ironically, Jerry Nolan had taught Peter Criss, the drummer from Kiss, to play back in Brooklyn and Arthur found a drinking buddy in Ace Frehley, their guitarist.

Behind the scenes, Steve Leber, Marty Thau and Irwin Steinberg were finally doing business. On March 20, The New York Dolls signed a two album deal with Mercury. The record company put up a $25,000 advance and an allowance for new equipment, while the band's weekly wage was increased to $200 per Doll. In reality, Mercury was a second rung label with a solid, conservative reputation whose star turn was Rod Stewart (as a solo performer but not with The Faces). Taking on the Dolls was the most radical move Mercury Records ever made and they got a preview of what to expect when Marty Thau and Paul Nelson took David Johansen to Chicago to meet the senior team. Marty Thau: "The night before we left for Chicago, David had been out on the town. He was staying over at Barbara Troiani's house and they had got back at six in the morning, drunk out of their heads. I showed up at eight with a limousine. David was still drunk and Barbara was at the sewing machine putting the finishing touches to what he was going to wear to the meeting. We get to Chicago and are taken into this boardroom with the largest table I've ever seen in my life, then in comes Irwin Steinberg, Mike Gormley from publicity and all these heads of departments that we've never met before. It was a really important meeting to determine how we could utilise David to be a voice to the press when all of a sudden he leans forward, his head smashes down on the table and he's fallen asleep." What was left of the meeting was punctuated by sleeping beauty's snoring.

The Dolls, with the help of Bob Gruen, attempted to make amends by sending a tape of the band to the senior Mercury staff in Chicago. It was a well intentioned gesture that also fell flat on its face. Bob Gruen: "They played at Max's one night and we made this ten minute reel in the dressing room. It was funny, they were pretending they were talking to people in the boardroom. David, because he knew the layout of Mercury's boardroom, was going: 'Hi, how are you?' to the president, and, 'We've got the muscle if you've got the hustle.' It was all very loose and very drunk. Now in those days people didn't have reel-to-reel machines to show tapes in their office, it was all new. We had wanted them to be able to set it up in some casual place but they had to rent a studio in a technology lab. All these executives had to leave the office and sit in a screening room to watch this outrageous 3am drunken debauched dressing room scene. They were so shocked."

Uppermost on the Dolls' agenda was finding a producer capable of capturing their volatile spirit. Mention was made of Phil Spector but the idea came to nothing. David Bowie declined due to pressing engagements, while Leiber and Stoller, the legendary songwriting team responsible for such gems as 'Jailhouse Rock', 'Hound Dog' and 'Riot In Cell Block Number 9', said they would rather produce the Dolls' second album. The former leader of The Move, Roy Wood, who had imbued his latest band, Wizzard, with a Phil Spector sound and could duplicate the glories of The Ronettes and Dion with apparent ease, was also considered. Unfortunately, Wood was unable to offer his services as he was going through a nervous breakdown. Todd Rundgren wasn't an initial choice but he was available and had notched up studio experience working with The Band and Badfinger. Rundgren also looked the part with his multi-coloured hair and satin suits but despite his appearance he was a strict taskmaster when it came to making music. Apart from being friendly with Rundgren's model girlfriend, Bebe Buell, the Dolls knew little about him but some demos done at Todd's home studio showed enough promise for them to proceed with a working relationship. Rundgren told *Creem*: "The only person who can logically produce a New York City record is someone who lives in New York. I live here, and I recognise all the things about New York that the Dolls recognise in their music. It doesn't necessarily mean that I testify to that stuff, it doesn't mean that the Dolls' music testifies to that stuff. The only thing that it testifies to is that they're punks!"

The Dolls, their producer, girlfriends, crew, cronies and press pals entered Studio B of the Record Plant on 44th Street. Rundgren didn't like having to contend with the band's seven day weekend work ethic or their entourage but they didn't complain when his dog peed on the mixing desk, either. Cyrinda Foxe: "They hadn't had much experience in the studio so they didn't know what to ask for but it was a lot of fun. Everything that they ever did was a photo session and that's the way it went in the studio. I got into a garter belt and fishnet stockings and started posing, while Betty Thau took photos. The Dolls were a cartoon rock'n'roll band like The Monkees . . . completely animated."

Their high spirits were further enhanced by the prerequisite liquor and hash, plus cocaine which would have increased their brash flash approach. The Dolls and their friends apparently terrified James Taylor's brother, Livingston, who was diligently recording with a string quartet in the studio next door. Rundgren concocted a rocky avalanche of sound under which some of the Dolls felt muffled. Jerry Nolan, whose forthright drumming kept the band in check, complained to Thau during the making of the album. Marty: "Rundgren was cold and indifferent. He didn't exhibit any great enthusiasm although he meant business and was very serious. He worked hard on it but that absence of communication was not well received. He didn't bother with them in any way and they didn't like him for it. Jerry Nolan came to me and said, 'I don't think he's portraying my drum sound or the presence of my drums correctly.' Everybody wants to be properly represented at any recording but I listened to Jerry and what they had done and I did think that maybe the drums could be more forceful. I mentioned it to Todd, he was at the board and he turned to me and said, 'How dare you, this is my drum sound and I've been using it successfully for many years.' He didn't have to respond in such a fashion."

If Rundgren was curt and reserved, the Dolls were a wild rabble, demanding to be heard individually and larking round with their entourage. Johansen was so drunk he can't remember anything about the recording sessions, while Johnny attempted to break the sound barrier. Sylvain, always the mediator in the band, kept a semblance of melody flowing between Thunders' flurries of squawking riffs. He didn't have a problem working with Rundgren. Sylvain: "Jesus Christ couldn't have done a better job, dealing with five guys all going, 'Hey listen to me, put him down and put me up and fuck them.' Johansen couldn't see it as a whole, with everybody contributing. Because of my style which was a clean rhythm with more open chords, I was getting drowned out by Johnny who was fighting sound with sound. The thing that was most screwed up, though, was Mercury rushed Todd and maybe it's the mix that Jerry wasn't happy with."

The New York Dolls were the purest form of rock'n'roll and they invoked the kind of energy that can't be sustained without damaging the hosts and is virtually impossible to distil for mass consumption. Rundgren was faced with a hopeless task but although there was a distinct lack of rapport between him and the band, the end result was no horror story.

Their eponomously titled début album – Johnny Thunders

had suggested they call it *The New York Dolls' Greatest Hits* – was only marginally polished in production and the band retained their city grime. 'Personality Crisis' is embellished by Todd's tinkling piano arrangement and 'Looking For A Kiss' opens with a homage to the boy's heroines, The Shangri-Las. 'Jet Boy' becomes a frantic sabre dance with Johnny and Sylvain letting rip while Johansen howls in the background. Rundgren's best work on the album was in emphasising the Dolls' backing vocals.

All the 'Oohs' and 'Woawoahs' which recalled Sixties girl groups were fully utilised, especially on 'Trash' which was intended to be their first single. Written by Sylvain and David Jo, 'Trash' is both cute and savage. Drenched in Dolly histrionics from Sylvain's teen angel background vocals to the punchy rhythm section, it is chock full of Johansen's imaginative flaky lyrics which perfectly evoke Dolly locations and emotions: 'I'll go to Lover's Leap with you/I'll go to Planet Blue with you/I'll go to Fairyland with you' . . . but . . . 'Please don't ask me if I love you/Because I don't know if I do', while Thunders batters the melody line completely out of shape. Only the hardest of hearts could fail to be moved by it, which seemed to be the majority of the record buying public. On its release in July, 'Trash' b/w 'Personality Crisis' made little impression on the charts.

Although usually not given to songwriting, Arthur Kane contributed his plea for sanity with 'Private World'. Arthur: "It's about being able to get away, whether you go for a ride in your car or barricade yourself in a room, take drugs, whatever. It's a fantasy place. We were Dolls 24 hours a day. You couldn't hang up your Dolls suit and go play golf! Then when the fans located us, it became crazy. They knew where we lived and where we hung out. There were always people around us, we were never protected but it's something that we did to ourselves." Opening with a steady bass run that is accosted by a riff akin to nails scraping down a blackboard, Johansen then announces 'Breakdown . . . to a private world', revealing Kane practically hiding under his bed from all the commotion.

Arthur: "We were no longer just teenagers out having fun. We were in the business now. I started getting this railroaded feeling even before the album came out."

Older numbers like 'Frankenstein', 'Bad Girl', 'Subway Train' and the albums only cover, 'Pills', were all fully realised while 'Lonely Planet Boy', which was written by Johansen before he joined the Dolls, slows down the normally rapid pace. The Dolls never had a handle on subtlety and the record's one vaguely quiet moment barely contains their energy. Johansen's thick accent and gravel tones aren't really equipped to deal with matters of poignancy but it was always the band's flaws that made them so naturally charming. Augmented in the studio by Buddy Bowser's scratchy sax playing and Sylvain's lost in space trilling, 'Lonely Planet Boy' became a regular part of the Dolls' on-stage acoustic interludes. 'Vietnamese Baby' was David Johansen's brave attempt at political comment. Whereas Iggy Pop used images of the Vietnam War to further project himself in 'Search & Destroy', Johansen focuses on the indifference of those in power. Sylvain: "These were the days of Search and Destroy units going out there and massacring whole villages. The news back home wasn't very pleasant to watch on television and this was Johansen's reflection of the political scene in the early Seventies. The music is not the most important part of that song but we did a pretty good job of deciphering what he wanted from his guitar playing. His fingernails would get caught between the strings."

There wasn't enough time to record 'Babylon', a relatively new, loose and leery crowd pleaser. Not a biblical metaphor, Babylon is four stops past Amityville on the Long Island railroad. Johansen explained to the music press that "Babylon is about people who live in Babylon, Long Island, New York, who go into the city every night dressed to kill. These people have to get home before sun-up, you know, like vampires that can't get caught by the sun. This girl finally splits Babylon and moves to Manhattan where she gets a job in a massage parlour." The Dolls were rushed out of the studio to begin their live commitments before Rundgren finished the final mixes with Mercury Records breathing down his neck.

For the album cover, Mercury organised an unbecoming photo shoot of the band in a Third Avenue antique shop, surrounded by moose heads, stop signs and various curios. Sylvain: "We did our own make-up, we didn't have a make-up artist or anything. It was two o'clock in the afternoon which is not a very good time to meet the Dolls if you want a picture of them. We take the pictures and then we have a meeting to decide which photograph to use for the cover, but between a massive array of antiques, your tight pants or even your face aren't exactly going to stand out. To me, it was a piece of shit. Whaddaya mean, this is going to be my album cover? I got thrown out of Egypt for this? Mercury was telling us that it was too late to do anything else."

The Dolls were given two days to come up with a finished alternative. Sylvain enlisted the help of two fashion designers, Pinky and Diane, who in turn recruited a *Vogue* fashion photographer called Toshi and his partner Shin, a hairdresser. Toshi's Park Avenue loft became the site of the shoot and a ratty old couch, which was hastily covered in white satin, became the main prop. The final sleeve, still one of the most notorious in rock history, had an intended element of parody. If every notion regarding the Dolls was already exaggerated, why not take it even further? Sylvain: "Shin did our hair and threw in some hair pieces for the bouffants, not that Johnny needed it. Then this guy who was a drag queen but also worked in fashion did the make-up and went all out on us. Johansen just wanted more and more. I wanted to look like a Raggedy Annie mannequin and because I knew everybody else was going to wear platforms, I thought I'd wear my roller skates. Johnny was wear a red and black dungaree jacket, a kid's jacket, and black stretch lamé pants. Sometimes we used to wear kid's clothing, we could fit into them 'cos we were so emaciated. We had no food!"

If colours can clash, then the colour shots taken at the session were an all-out rainbow rumble. In the end a black and white picture of the band sitting pretty on the couch was used for the cover. At their feet are a couple of casually thrown items: a can of Schlitz beer is emasculated by the straw sticking out of it, a most useful device for preventing smudged lipstick when slurping. Next to the beer is a dainty little purse and an open pack of Lucky Strikes, with a torn corner and a cheap lighter. All pretty insignificant stuff but the cigarettes carry a secret code. Sylvain: "Everything has a meaning. There's a gay message that David did with the Lucky Strikes. How the cigarettes were indicated sexual preference, in the same way that guys would wear their keys in either their right or left back trouser pocket or by the colour of their bandannas but when you send out the wrong signals everything begins to go wrong."

The Dolls look like a gang of murderous queens, the kind that hide razor blades in their mouths to use when French kissing. David Jo was typically blithe: "I look like Simone Signoret, Johnny looks like Anna Magnani, Jerry looks like Lee Remick, Syl looks like Polly Bergen and Arthur's got a Dietrich thing going on."

It was a fabulous statement but like so many of the things The New York Dolls did, it caused them untold damage. They knew they were breaking down barriers but they didn't understand how deeply rooted prejudice can be. Paul Nelson: "I never expected the cover to be that controversial. I remember being at one of the top FM stations in Philadelphia with the record and some guy there just went on and on about the cover, saying how he would never play it because of that. I didn't expect leading radio stations to be shocked by it, it didn't seem that shocking to me. I guess familiarity with their persona made me immune to the fact that they were going to be judged on the cover, by itself. It created something that remained at the forefront of a lot of people's opinions, and they never got beyond the cover."

6

Little L.A. Women

The New York Dolls' début album was released in the US on July 27, 1973, and began a hesitant journey into chart territory. Most of the music critics adored it. Bud Scoppa in his review for *Penthouse* wrote: "The Dolls are a vicious kick in the face to all that's careful, passive and polished about today's popular music. The record companies, most of which have a great investment in exactly the kind of music the Dolls are rallying against, have naturally been turned off." Nick Kent, *NME*'s doyen of decadence, was also hot-to-trot: "The New York Dolls are trash, they play rock'n'roll like sluts and they've just released a record that can stand beside Iggy & The Stooges' stupendous *Raw Power* as the only album so far to fully define just exactly where 1970s rock should be coming from."

The niche that The New York Dolls carved out for themselves never really got that much bigger, even when they landed a record deal. Although Johansen predicted that, "The kids will love us", the majority didn't and instead went out and bought *Goat's Head Soup*, the new and rather lacklustre album by the Stones. As Paul Nelson noted in the *Village Voice*: "They (the Dolls) were unquestionably brilliant, but finally too spare, too restricted, to reach the hidden places in suburban, small-town hearts. In the end, they rode on real rather than symbolic subway trains to specific rather than universal places, played for an audience of intellectuals or kids ever farther out than they were: and when they eventually met the youth of the country, that youth seemed even more confused than captivated by them."

On July 28, the Dolls appeared at the Tiger Stadium in

Massilon, Ohio, playing the first of several support slots to Mott The Hoople, who were riding on the success of 'All The Young Dudes', a gift from Bowie. While the band were out of town, the Mercer Arts Center was reduced to rubble when The Broadway Central Hotel collapsed on top of it. Leee Childers: "Do you know the story of the boy from Iowa or somewhere, who was in the Mercer Arts Center and he decided to phone his mother? He said, 'Hi mom, I just wanted to let you know that I arrived . . .' and that's when the Mercer Arts Center fell down, unfortunately for this particular boy. If it had happened at night, when there was a band performing and a whole crowd of people dancing, we would have all been killed."

While the Dolls were limbering up for an August 3 slot at New York's Felt Forum, once again supporting Mott The Hoople, Mercury Records dealt the band an underhand blow by signing Bachman-Turner Overdrive. Hailing from Canada, Bachman-Turner Overdrive played radio friendly blues rock and looked like real men with real beards and Levi jeans. Furthermore, leader Randy Bachman was a devout Mormon who banned alcohol from the group's dressing room. Here was a band Mercury could appreciate and they accorded them all the favours they eventually withheld from the Dolls. Still, the Felt Forum gig looked like it was going to be one of the summer's big events. Located within Madison Square Garden, with an audience capacity of 5,000, the show promised to be special.

While one would have considered the gig something of a glitter bug's ball, the Dolls' fans were vastly outnumbered by a crowd wearing the standard concert-going uniform of blue denim and rock logo T-shirts. Legendary DJ Murray The K welcomed Todd Rundgren who came out from the wings to introduce the Dolls wearing a gold lamé suit and bouncing a giant beach ball. Sylvain: "We ran on that stage in the same way that The Rolling Stones did on the TAMI show in California. We went into 'Courageous Cat' and the crowd went nuts." Built on a variation of the instrumental 'Peter Gunn', the

'Courageous Cat' theme was lifted from a children's cartoon show that Johnny and Syl were partial to watching on TV. The band had also begun covering The Shangri-La's 'Give Him A Great Big Kiss' which offered Johnny the opportunity to sidle up to the mike to ask David Jo, in his inimitable Queens' twang, 'Well, how does she dance?' The retort is immortal: 'Close, very, very close.'

Resplendent in top hat and white bib, Johansen showered the first couple of rows with fizzing Moet & Chandon before the Dolls made way for Mott. The *NME*'s New York correspondent, Linda Solomon, was not impressed . . . "A tape of rush hour traffic noises served as a warning for what was to come. Out pranced the Dolls like a plague of locusts, punching in with 'Personality Crisis' from their new album. The band blew themselves out in their first five minutes. After going nowhere on the mouth harp during 'Pills', Johansen, whose sense of humour eludes me, shouted, 'If you're a garbage pail in the house, stick out your can!' Distinct cries of, 'We want Mott!' were audible and being neither a garbage pail nor a child, I couldn't have agreed more."

At the aftershow party held in the Green Tulip room of the Plaza Hotel, a bare chested Iggy Pop showed off some of the scabby self-inflicted wounds acquired during his recent set at Max's, while Todd and Bebe posed for pictures, and Wayne County wore little paper cutouts in his hair, advertising The Dave Clark Five. The Dolls and Sly Stone, meanwhile, were embroiled in a heated discussion with the hotel's stuffy security, who were refusing to let anyone through, even friends, without party passes. It was a far cry from the slack etiquette they were used to at the Mercer Arts Center.

On August 7, the concert-going citizens of Wilkensberg, Pennsylvania, got their chance to see the Dolls at the Alpine Arena. The band's next set of dates, August 14, 15, and 16, were closer to home, at My Father's Place, in Roslyn, Long Island. Back in Manhattan, Sylvain took David, Johnny and Arthur to a fashion fair at the Macalpine Hotel, where he introduced them to

Malcolm McLaren and Vivienne Westwood. Sylvain had been into Let It Rock, Malcolm and Vivienne's Kings Road shop, which focused on a hard-core Teddy Boy look, during his solo trip to London, but prior to the fashion fair, there was no other connection between the Dolls and McLaren. Malcolm: "We went to New York for a boutique show. It was the opening of a whole new line, we were moving away from Teddy Boys and creating our own clothes. We were suddenly modernising and becoming quite expressionistic with torn T-shirts. I used to get cigarettes and burn holes in girls' blouses, there was a destructive element to it. We hung them up in this boutique stand and not one single American buyer was interested. The only people who came into our room was The New York Dolls and a couple of other people like Alice Cooper."

Intrigued by the Dolls and NY's underground scene, Malcolm began to study the band in their natural habitat at Max's, but he didn't fall in love until he heard them rock'n'roll, when David put on the album for him. Malcolm: "When I heard it, I just fell over backwards. I thought my God, this is so bad, how could they make a record like that? I was absolutely shocked and it made me laugh. It made me laugh so much that I suddenly thought that you can be brilliant at being bad and there were people loving them for it. I loved them from that moment on. I was sold, hook, line and sinker and I loved the photograph of them on the album cover, sitting on the couch. I loved that asexual or bi-sexual look which in many ways had a direct correlation with much of what had happened in English pop but Vivienne and I liked it much better because we thought it was somewhat cruder and tougher. They were in many respects inspiring for us."

McLaren and Westwood were staying at the Chelsea Hotel and threw a little party in honour of the Dolls before they returned to London. Punch prepared in a Greek delicatessen was served, accompanied by bowls of Hula-hoops, and they decorated the room with all their unsold wares. Peter Jordan: "They had some great things, Jerry Lee Lewis underpants . . . 'The Killer is Back' underwear, and all these English style

Fifties shirts, like Billy Fury or Adam Faith would have worn. Plus they scattered these old soft core lingerie magazines around. We went up there and stole everything we could get our hands on. Malcolm thought New York was great, he was really into it. In comparison to Soho, where if you're Lord Snooty you might get some warm champagne and see a bit of skirt, in New York you'll see a male hooker with no pants on. He was the most naïve little guy. 'Ooh Pete is that really a guy in a dress, ooh' but he had a lot of enthusiasm and he wasn't a dope. He could design a pair of shoes in an instant, you'd tell him what you wanted and it would be in the mail from England in four days."

Malcolm left his heart behind when he went home to launch the latest incarnation of his King's Road shop Too Fast To Live, Too Young To Die with Vivienne Westwood. "London seemed so dull in comparison, but we'd opened the new store and we carried on working. Some loose inspiration began to appear in our clothes, funny little grey T-shirts with holes in them started to get more fluffy and glam, a liftoff from those days in New York."

Following a stand at Max's from August 22–27, the Dolls had a day off scheduled before they were due to fly out to Los Angeles, where they had a five night booking at the Whisky A Go Go on Sunset Strip. The LA glitterati were buzzing about the band's imminent arrival and all the groupie girls who sashayed along the Strip in little more than lingerie had feverish expectations. Especially the delectable 15-year-old Sabel Starr (nee Shields), the uncrowned queen of the scene, who after seeing a photo of the Dolls in *Creem* magazine set her sights on Johnny Thunders. Sabel wasn't the only one who scanned the rock rags for talent. Sylvain: "There were two magazines, on the East Coast we used to get *Rock Scene*, and on the West Coast there was *Star* magazine, which used to feature all the Hollywood starlets. Me and Johnny used to get import copies of *Star* and there'd be pictures of Sabel Starr in it, and

Johnny used to say, 'Wow, this girl Sabel, I love her. When I go out to LA she'll be my girlfriend.' "

Trouble came looming, however, with a knife in her hand, when Arthur's girlfriend, Connie Gripp, attacked him two days before the band were due to depart for LA. Even at the best of times, theirs was a flammable relationship, generously marinated in alcohol. Peter Jordan: "Connie was a dancer and a hooker. She was a girl with a big ass, a big laugh and a big mouth. She was a nice person but a lost soul. Arthur had the ability to attract these types of girls to him. Out of all the people in the band, he was the one most into the Times Square night life, the sleazier side. He wasn't a sadist or a masochist. He wasn't a leather freak or a whore but he had a knack of pulling people in like that and Connie was of that milieu."

When Connie pulled her Lady MacBeth stunt, in their 2nd Street and First Avenue apartment, Arthur was out cold and at his most vulnerable. Arthur: "She wanted to go to California with the group and it just wasn't in the scheme of things with the managers. They weren't going to buy tickets for people's girlfriends. We'd just played ten shows at Max's, two a day and I was very tired, stoned, been drinking all the time. I came home, it was very late and I went to sleep. I was lying face down and I heard something. She was standing on top of me holding a kitchen knife, so then I tried to stand up and take it away from her but she'd tied my ankles together. I tried to get the knife away from her and she cut my hand. Then I got mad so I thought whatever's going to happen, I have to get the knife away from her, I managed to wrestle it away but somehow in the process, I sliced my hand open and the bone was hanging out. Then she, with no clothes, went out on the front fire escape. She was a great one for climbing out on the fire escape in the middle of winter with no clothes on. She had an outrageous body. This is the same girl who for kicks would take her clothes off and go out on the avenue and pretend she was hitchhiking, then watch the cars crash."

With 85 cents in his pocket, Arthur left Connie on the fire escape and unsteadily made his way out on to the street to hail a cab, leaving a trail of blood behind him. He was patched up at Bellevue hospital and unable to play for two months. Although Kane was musically incapacitated, the band still took him on tour. Peter Jordan: "We couldn't leave him in New York because we were worried that he would kill himself. Out of all the people in the band, he was probably the most close to the street. His life was like, 'Where do I sleep tonight?' " Jordan deputised for the Dolls' injured bassist throughout the tour, although Arthur would still be present on stage during the shows, standing mournfully to one side, his lower arm in a cast, like a bizarre exhibit. A rumour grew that Peter Jordan, hidden behind the amps would regularly cover for Kane when he was too drunk to play. This only happened once however, on the *Midnight Special* TV show because Arthur was still plastered up.

Tickets for the forthcoming Dolls shows at the Whisky were snapped up within three hours of going on sale and the guest list was reported to be even longer than the lines of people who had waited for the club's small ticket office to open. Sabel Starr had ascertained that the Dolls would be staying at the Continental Hyatt House on Sunset, although it was hardly a revelation as most of the bands that passed through Hollywood stayed at the hotel now known in rock circles as the Riot House. When the Dolls pulled up outside the hotel in their limos, Sabel and a girlfriend presented them with gifts purchased from a sex shop. Sabel: "We got them all something. Syl got some crotchless underwear, David this cocksucker thing and I got Johnny some silver Frederick's of Hollywood underwear, which was my favourite. I gave Johnny his present and he goes, 'Why don't you come upstairs up with me?' It was so weird because I knew he was going to be mine. For a week we never left that room, we fell in love instantly. I was fifteen, he'd just turned 21. Marty Thau was outraged. 'Johnny, you can't do this, she's only 15!' He said, 'Marty, I'm

91

going to marry her.' He phoned his mother and said, 'I'm bringing this girl home and I'm going to marry her.' "

Johnny and Janis Cafasso had gone their separate ways after Thunders' neediness turned to violence but to the enraptured Miss Starr, the Dolls' lead guitarist embodied all her rock'n'roll dreams. The attraction was mutual. Sylvain: "Johnny and Sabel went in to the hotel bedroom. She gives him a blow job and that's it, they were married in the eyes of God. He was hers and she was his." Sabel was one of the loosest Lolitas on the scene but she had a charming candour and the beguiling appearance of a cheerleader turned teen tramp. Raised with her sister, Corel, in the exclusive neighbourhood of Palos Verdes, the two girls hit the Strip and notched up some impressive scores between them. Corel was whisked off by Robert Plant while Sabel got Jimmy Page. Then there was T. Rex, Mott The Hoople and David Bowie to name but a few of the acts they headlined. By the time The New York Dolls got into town, Corel was in a steady relationship with Iggy Pop, who often went back to the girls' house in Palos Verdes for dinner with their mom, and up to the family's holiday cabin. Pop later showed his appreciation by writing the vile 'Rich Bitch', apparently about Corel ... 'Now when your mama's too old to buy you pills/And your daddy ain't around to pay your bills/And your cunt's so big you could drive through a truck/And every man you meet baby/He knows you sure being fucked'. Wonder what Pop wrote on his valentines?

With Corel out of circulation, Sabel continued with her exploits and was making quite a name for herself. In her memoirs *I'm With The Band* Pamela Des Barres, then Pamela Miller, describes being ousted from her position as queen of the rock courtesans by Sabel and her foxy friends ... "The rock and roll girls were getting younger, and I was no good at competing. They hated me because I had been there first, and they called me awful names at Rodney Bingenheimer's English Disco, 'old' being the most popular odious declaration of loathing ... The most hideous of these tartlets was Sable Starr.

She thought she invented nipples and pubic hair." Sabel's standard wardrobe was little more than a garter belt, stockings and heels but after falling for Johnny, she announced her retirement from groupiedom at the Whisky.

The Dolls' five night run at The Whisky became legendary before they even played a note, and it forever changed the face of LA's rock scene. If the band was even more shambolic than usual, it mattered not to the under-age boys and girls in their garish gladrags who lined the perimeter of the stage, then after each show fought, milk tooth and varnished nail to get backstage. David Johansen told *Creem*: "It was amazing. I didn't think they let children like that out at night. If you could have seen it from where I was standing, little kids grabbing at me; literally they couldn't have been more than twelve years old. Little boys with lipstick . . . and they would touch my legs and my hands. I loved it. Those kids just wanted to be a part of the pandemonium."

On stage or off, The New York Dolls lived in continuous performance, rock'n'roll was their vocation, not a career. With so many distractions, they neglected working on new material and their live repertoire had barely changed since the Mercer Arts Center, with the exceptions of 'Who Are The Mystery Girls?', a failed candidate for their début LP, and a cover of The Cadets' 1956 novelty number 'Stranded In The Jungle', which they introduced into their set after Billy died. 'Mystery Girls' is a terse outburst concerning the misuse of love . . . 'Who's the one who wants to kick it on the floor/And try to beat it like a scatter rug?' Cupid is duly chastened by some scourging guitar dispatches and a pummelling rhythm section. 'Stranded' follows the fortunes of a poor guy trying to get back to his girlfriend in the States after his plane crashes in the jungle. Distinctly split between the city and the wilderness, it was playtime for the Dolls, complete with jungle drums, animal noises and Johansen's attempt at a chest beating baritone.

To get thrown out of the musician-tolerant Hyatt House was just another of those rare accolades bestowed upon the band during their stay in LA. Unlike Led Zeppelin, who swept into town like a marauding horde, there was no real brutality in the Dolls' antics. As true hedonists they were so involved in the pursuit of pleasure they rarely wasted time on cruelty, except for the baloney incident, which probably prompted the band's enforced departure from the Hyatt. Leee Childers: "There was this groupie who was really being pushy and annoying. Apparently she was behaving really badly so they put her in a chair, naked. Then they wrapped her in tape, taped her to the chair so she couldn't get out, then they covered her naked body with slices of baloney, presumably because that's what was at hand. It could have been ham or prosciutto but it happened to be baloney. They carried the whole taped package out, put it in the elevator and punched for the lobby. The doors closed and down she went. Then the doors opened in the hotel lobby and there was a naked girl covered in baloney."

The Dolls were swamped by female attention. Like a Roman Polanski wet dream, long-limbed babes with downy thighs and kohl-black eyes made themselves forever available. Jerry Nolan, who was still adjusting to being a Doll, was in wonderland. Sylvain: "Jerry was still new in the Dolls. He was very happy and if he got a girl, forget it, to him that was a peach."

This being Hollywood, even the star-struck moms got in on the act by living vicariously through their teenage daughters. Sylvain: "Hollywood in the early Seventies was really crazy. These trash Hollywood mothers in their leopardskin slips started throwing their daughters at us. There's this one photograph (by Bob Gruen) where our groupies are lying down on the floor in front of us, and we're practically stepping on them, while their mothers were standing right there going 'Get on the floor!'."

The Dolls relocated to the Ramada Inn, a pleasant if typical two-storey Hollywood hotel built around the swimming pool area. Amongst the palm trees and sun loungers, the revellers began to gather, waiting for the band to emerge from their rooms, the newly crowned heads of LA's lotus eaters. Little starlets shimmied around Iggy and The Stooges, who basked by the poolside like cold-blooded cobras. Groupies cooed over heart-throb David Cassidy's younger and cuter brother, Shaun. Someone opened a bottle for Arthur, his hand still in plaster, and David adjusted his white boob tube and wondered where all the real movie stars had gone. Then a roadie knocked a box of washing powder into the swimming pool, and suddenly it was a bubble bath party. The following day the Dolls were kicked out of the Ramada Inn.

Johnny Thunders was absent from much of the carousing, preferring to spend every possible moment with his bride-to-be. So busy were they staring into each others' eyes that Sabel and Johnny managed to get busted for jaywalking across Hollywood Boulevard and were ordered to pay a fine to the traffic division of the juvenile court. Sabel: "Johnny was so sweet and innocent and so cute. That first week was magical. I just fell in love with him. During the day we'd hang around Hollywood Boulevard, we went to all the shops and we got our picture taken in a little photo booth, it was so much fun. Johnny and I just went off on our own, then there'd be the gigs at night. I thought I'd died and gone to heaven." Johnny and Sabel started hanging out with Iggy and Corel. While the Shields girls giggled and gossiped about how they were going to have the wildest double wedding in rock'n'roll history, Pop took Thunders to one side and it wasn't for lessons in marriage etiquette. Sylvain: "Johnny was a big Iggy Pop fan and the four of them were always together and one thing led to another. Johnny's the kind of guy, you turn him onto one joint and the next day he's got a whole pound, so they fix together and that's when that started. Johnny began using, not regularly at first, just a little bit here and a little bit there. It turned out to be the worst thing you could ever introduce Johnny to, with all his problems, all the sexual confusion, 'Am I a boy or a girl?' Heroin was perfect 'cos it puts you at rest with all that."

Iggy had taken another virgin with his metal wand and magic powder. Meanwhile, Leee Childers had been dispatched to Hollywood to watch over Pop on behalf of MainMan. Leee: "Iggy set out to turn people on to heroin. I don't know for sure what his reasons were but I lived with him for eight or nine months and I watched him do it. We had this really nice big house in the Hollywood Hills, he was with Corel then, and he'd invite people up to the house. It gave him something in his head, it was like sex I guess, he'd tie them off and shoot 'em up, watch the blood bloom in the syringe. Watch them have their first high and that's what he got off on."

The New York Dolls left LA for San Francisco where on September 5 and 6 they had two shows at the Matrix with The Tubes in support. They returned to the City of Angels for a couple of TV appearances, live on the *Midnight Special*, with Peter Jordan behind the amplifiers, and miming two numbers on *The Real Don Steele Show*, a local programme that featured dancing girls and showbiz gossip.

As the next leg of the tour took the Dolls down south, Johnny packed Sabel off to New York. Cyrinda Foxe was already out in Texas on a modelling assignment and had arranged to meet up with the band at the airport. Cyrinda: "I got there first and I'm sitting there waiting for them, when I see all these burly state troopers and I could see they were looking at me. The Texas rangers are really scary, you don't mess with them, they have a reputation for killing so I was frightened to death. It became more and more apparent that I was of interest to them, then this woman ranger stepped forward and I knew they were there for me."

Unbeknown to Cyrinda, Sabel Starr's mother had informed the police that her daughter had run off with Johnny Thunders of The New York Dolls. The Texas Rangers had been told to intercept a young, slender blonde and they held Cyrinda for questioning until she could prove her identity. On arrival in New York, Sabel called her mom and convinced her to turn off the heat on the band. While Mrs Shields cooled

Wear Truth and Soul
and you can hang up your flag.

Truth and Soul™ fashions do what the flag used to do for your wardrobe. And everybody is wearing them except the flag bearer.

But he'll get his. In tweeds, stripes, ribs or suedes. There are 22 hip sweater styles that are turning everybody on.

Truth and Soul, baby. It's honest. It's wild. It's color. It's cool. It's love in a far out line of threads. It's the revolution in fashion.

And you don't have to salute it to dig it.

Seek Truth and Soul.

Truth and Soul Fashions, 691 Broadway, N.Y.C.
Guaranteed for one full year's normal wear, refund or replacement when returned with tag and sales slip to Monsanto. 100% Acrilan® acrylic.

An advert for Truth and Soul – the funky fashion outlet that Syl and Billy originally set up, circa 1969, before selling out to the Nausbaum Knitting Mills in Brooklyn. (Courtesy of Sylvain Mizrahi archives.)

Sylvain and Billy – walking in a winter wonderland, New York 1968.
(Picture by Alphonso Murcia, used courtesy of the Sylvain Mizrahi archives.)

Blonde Bombedshells – Rick Rivets and Arthur Kane, 1970.

Dolly Daydreams – Johnny Thunders, early 1971. (Leee Childers)

David Johansen and Thunders – mouth to mouth, but not always eye to eye.
(Leee Childers)

Smouldering Billy M – "a cool drink of water with a hot head".
(Leee Childers)

Hot pants and hot licks. Syl and Arthur get it on, early 1971.
(Leee Childers)

Cyrinda Foxe, a beautiful blonde Warhol ingenue –
"Andy wanted to marry me off to a banker". (Leee Childers)

Hearse rental – photo opp; Heathrow airport, October '72, one week before
Billy succumbs to a death worse than fate.

From hoodlum to harlot – Jerry 'I knew all the dirty tricks' Nolan.
(Bob Gruen)

"The Dolls were a cartoon rock 'n' roll band like the Monkees... completely animated" – Cyrinda Foxe. (Bob Gruen)

Hollywood Honeymooners – Johnny and Sabel Starr backstage at the Whisky, late August '73. (Bob Gruen)

David Jo and Todd Rundgren work on their ventriloquist act, backstage at The Felt Forum, August 3rd 1973. (Bob Gruen)

Calamity Kane and Saucy Syl. (Bob Gruen)

Johnny and Iggy Pop – a fix and a kiss. September '73.
(Courtesy of Peter Jordan)

Frenchy – valet of the Dolls greets Tommy the ticket lady from the 82 Club.
(Bob Gruen)

David Johansen – 'A prima ballerina on a spring afternoon'

The Brides of Frankenstein take to the road. (Bob Gruen)

Appearing on the Real Don Steele Show, September '73. (Bob Gruen)

"The worst striptease rock act you can imagine" – Malcolm MacLaren; Peter Jordan, Kane's stunt double, next to Arthur. (Bob Gruen)

The Lipstick Killers plotting the St Valentine's Day Mascara – at the Academy of Music, February 15 1974. (Bob Gruen)

Bosom Buddies – Johnny and David hanging out at Fredericks of Hollywood.
(Bob Gruen)

and Thau in ceremonial garb for the Dolls' Halloween bash at the Waldorf Astoria (Bob Gruen)

Big Mac and the Mighty Thau (Bob Gruen)

Hammered and Sick – the Dolls in the vinyl stages of their career at the Little Hippodrome, late Feb '75; Buddy Bowser on saxophone. (Bob Gruen)

Dolls' photo reunion, outside the Gem Spa, 1977. Photographer Roberta Bayley: " I remember asking David if he and Johnny were still friends and he said, 'C'mon, we went through the war together'."

down, the 'Mothers Of Memphis', a group of self-appointed moral guardians, were preparing to toast the Dolls like marshmallows in the flames of righteous indignity once the band got into town.

Their shows at Liberty Hall in Houston and Gurdey's in Dallas passed without incident but the Memphis moralists were laying in wait. As he sipped his coffee and flicked through the local papers *en route* to the Ellis Auditorium, David read the headlines of hate directed at the Dolls but considered it to be little more than inert hysteria. Marty Thau: "Before they went to Memphis, we were told that the police department and the Mothers Of Memphis felt that this was not a group to be seen – Mother's mind your children, keep them away from The New York Dolls, they are corrupt and evil. Well, naturally that kind of talk excited every kid in Memphis and the arena they were playing sold out in two minutes. It was packed out and in front of the stage there was a line of policemen holding clubs and standing to attention."

Iggy Pop opened for the Dolls that night, and couldn't have got arrested if he'd committed multiple murder on stage. No sir, those Billy clubs only started swinging once the Dolls came on. The riot was officially declared open when a boy broke through the cordon and planted a kiss on Johansen. David: "The cops started beating up the kids and I was trying to make them stop. I was saying stuff into the microphone like, 'That could be the mayor's son you're beating up on' and they hauled me away for inciting a riot."

The police also charged the Dolls' frontman with a lewd public behaviour rap, before putting him in steel bracelets and whisking him off to the jail house. David: "I'm sitting in the back of the police car in handcuffs, and I'm dressed like – oh forget it! – you do not want to go to jail in Memphis the way I was dressed. I was wearing these Norma Kamali pants, women's shoes and I'm like, Oh God . . . I'm going to jail. The whole thing was a set up, and I was so stupid, I mean I'd read it in the paper that they were going to get us. We were on Elvis

Presley boulevard and I said to the police, 'You wouldn't do this to Elvis Presley' and they said, 'We'd love to get him.' So then I had to get fingerprinted and they put me in a cell with three other guys who were sleeping. I tried to hide the way I was dressed by pulling this really raunchy old blanket up to my neck but one of the guys wakes up and comes over to look at me, and he goes, 'Holy shit, you're David Johansen!' So he wakes up this really big guy, huge, like a sisterfucker, and the first guy is going, 'Hey, do you know who that is?' and I'm like, 'Oh God!' but fortunately he left me alone. I got bailed out before I got into any trouble."

David was saved by the bail and on September 22 the Dolls skipped out of the South and on to Detroit where, before the band tore into 'Looking For A Kiss', Johansen announced from the stage of the Michigan Palace: "Well I spent last night in jail in Memphis and I been drunk all day so when I say I'm in love, you best *believe* I'm in love, motherfucker!"

Detroit loved The New York Dolls, and would go on loving them long after the rest of America had given up on them. The Dolls appealed to Detroit's innate fondness for renegade rock, the kind of pure adrenalin rush that had hitherto been delivered only by such home-grown bad boys as MC5 and Iggy and The Stooges. The tour continued without incident with dates in Milwaukee, Atlanta and West Palm Beach until they reached Chicago where Arthur attempted to play for the first time in weeks. It was a noble gesture, probably brought about by the fact that Chicago was the home of Mercury Records, but although he got through the set – in some discomfort – the effort set him back into plaster for at least ten more shows.

Next on the Dolls' itinerary, on October 13, was the Lion's Den in Missouri, where they were supported by hard-drinking, hard-living Dixie rockers Lynyrd Skynyrd. The two bands struck up an unlikely camaraderie. Peter Jordan: "Lynyrd Skynyrd had the dressing room next to us and they had one bottle of booze between them. We had about 12 bottles and we could hear them bitching so we invited them in. They'd thought we were a bunch of faggots but we wound up getting stoned drunk with them, had a ball. We had a good relationship with them ever after."

A gig in Rochester in upstate New York was followed on October 17 by a date at Kleinharts in Buffalo, where the venue owners had entered early into the spirit of Halloween, as did the Dolls' lead guitarist and front man. Sylvain: "I thought everything was going groovy on the tour until this one incident, but we were beginning to feel the pressure of being together every night. The stage had been dressed with a few carved pumpkins that were lit up from the inside with candles. There was one right in front of Jerry's beautiful pink drums. Johnny was a little bit out of it, he'd got hold of some speed and he and David had a spat over it. It wasn't a particularly good night. Sometimes the Dolls had their moments, other times they didn't, but it was only their spirits that brought them down. The magic of it being one unit, when we all wanted to play together as equals was when it gelled, but when we weren't feeling like that, it affected the performance. Johnny had finally told David he should cool it with his ego and that he wanted room to sing some songs. So they were already pissed off with each other anyway, when we went on stage. Johnny was facing Jerry. That whole night as far as I can remember, he played to Jerry, then he grabbed the pumpkin that was on the drum riser, swung it round by the stem and threw it up in the air, but he was still looking at Jerry, he didn't really know where he was throwing it. David was at the front, centre stage, looking at the audience and the worst fucking thing happened ... the damn pumpkin landed on David's head and smashed all over him, all over his beautiful little silk chemise, while he was doing his 'Do you think that you can make it with Frankenstein' thing. SPLATT! He got so fucking pissed."

They worked their way home with gigs in Boston, Philadelphia, St Louis, Minneapolis, Pittsburgh, Toronto and Bridgeport, Connecticut, before finally reaching New York on October 30. The following evening, all of Manhattan's children of the night made their way to the swish Waldorf Astoria Hotel for a rock'n'roll masquerade ball, featuring a Halloween costume competition that climaxed with a set by the Dolls. The doors to the Waldorf's Grand Ballroom were supposed to be thrown open at 11pm but a characteristic delay halted the proceedings until near midnight, by which time almost 1,000 fractious trick or treaters had gathered in the ballroom's narrow entrance, and sporadic fights between Dracula and King Kong versus Morticia and The Mummy began to worry the hotel management. Almost 2,000 angry partygoers were turned away when the guards began to separate the gate-crashers from the $7.50 ticket holders. The event finally got underway with the best costume competition which was judged by a select panel that included Rosemary Kent, editor of Andy Warhol's *Interview* magazine, Broadway star Tommy Tune and designer Chester Weinberg. After some deliberation, a silver skinned alien and an amazonian Mae West were jointly awarded the star prize – A Night On The Town with the Dolls. The second prize, a weekend for three at the Newark Motor Inn along with a bottle of New York State Champagne, was gratefully received by the runner up.

The Dolls missed their midnight stage cue by two hours but swiftly revived any flagging spirits in the Grand ballroom once they started their set. As usual, they leant heavily on well established material, save for a rendition of 'Lone Star Queen', a rough patchwork of Howlin' Wolf riffs which Johansen dedicated to Janis Joplin. In a review of the Waldorf gig, Ellen Willis, writing for the *New Yorker* noted that . . . "To know the Dolls' repertoire is to love it, but I've already heard it live half a dozen times and some fresh material would have been nice. The Dolls' next album, according to Johansen, is tentatively entitled 'Too Much Too Soon'. I hope so, but one new song per set is more likely too little, too late."

With just over two weeks to go before the Dolls embarked on a major European jaunt, there was little time for rest and recuperation. Sabel's lonely teardrops finally dried up once her rock'n'roll Romeo returned to her embrace but it was a short-lived reunion. Arthur was out of plaster and the band started rehearsing hard at Baggy's, a professional studio where they also stored their equipment. 'Nitebob', a.k.a. Bob Czaykowski, who had previously worked as The Stooge's soundman, joined the Dolls' crew. Peter Jordan: "We'd hit the point of being a professional band and started rehearsing on a fairly relentless basis. Through Baggy's we hooked up with some people who subsequently began working with us, specifically Nitebob, who became our sound mixer and was also a guitar and amplifier technician. He was almost solely responsible for the Dolls achieving what I consider to be the perfect sound, and there was a point when the Dolls were capable of being one of the top bands in the world."

Before leaving for Europe there were a few out of town dates to play, including one at Richard's in Atlanta, where Roy Hollingworth again caught up with them. His eloquence in the pages of *Melody Maker* revealed a touching devotion: "Here on this stage battles a baggage of balls and trousers and high-heeled shoes; and drunkenness and unwashed hair; and untuned guitars and songs that musicians would call a mess but a rock and roll child would say 'God Bless You – You are so necessary!' Rock and roll is sex. And the Dolls played on. And they played sex. Non-stop."

The young residents of Baltimore, Rhode Island, and New Jersey were similarly ravished. Europe was next and to mark The New York Dolls' return to the UK, *Melody Maker* gave over their front page to a particularly rumpled shot of the band in which Thunders is wearing a swastika armband on his black leather jacket. Appetites were certainly whetted but it was bile rather than eager anticipation that moved so many of its readers to send scathing letters of complaint to Britain's leading music paper.

7

A Hard Night's Day

Inextricably altered by time and experience, The New York Dolls returned to England on November 20, 1973. They even looked different from the feisty fledglings whose first UK tour had ended in tragedy. The once flirtatious bunch of second-hand roses in their thrift shop finery had been around the block and metamorphosed into hardened rock sluts with a penchant for satin and studs.

At the start of the band's itinerary, two possible television slots were pencilled in – a spot on the *Russell Harty Show*, a regional chat show, and an appearance on the cult-comedy show *Monty Python's Flying Circus* which regularly featured a bit of cross-dressing. The first confirmed sighting of the band, however, was at Warwick University on November 22. Two other university gigs followed at York and Leeds, where only 600 of the 2000 tickets had been sold. The Dolls were hardly cut out to entertain students in drab union halls at which decadence was measured by the amount of beer consumed, but they managed to break a little ice along the way. The tour coincided with the release of 'Jet Boy'/'Vietnamese Baby' and as the first album had only just been released in England, Mercury were hoping the visit would further bump up sales figures.

If The New York Dolls had seemed strange to their student audiences, then they were incomprehensible to Bob Harris, the mild-mannered television host of the *Old Grey Whistle Test*. Considered by its viewers to be a serious rock programme, the Dolls' inclusion on the show was a glorious deviation. Bob Harris smugly set himself up as a future figure of ignominy when he openly mocked the Dolls' performance of 'Jet Boy' and 'Looking For A Kiss'. For many a disenchanted youth, bored by the prevailing music scene, the band's appearance on the *Whistle Test* was a decisive moment. Up in Manchester Steven Morrissey, who would later collate the Dolls' press cuttings in an underground publication, wrote: "I was thirteen and it was my first real emotional experience". The Dolls were also crucial to the development of the early Sex Pistols. Paul Cook told Fred and Judy Vermorel: "I saw them (the Dolls) on the telly and I was fucking really knocked out by them. It was mainly their attitude I think. It was this really conventional BBC – you know the *Old Grey Whistle Test*. I couldn't believe it, they was just all falling about all over the place, all their hair down, all knocking into each other. Had these great big platform boots on. Tripping over. They was really funny. And they just didn't give a shit, you know. And Bob Harris at the end of it went: 'Tut, tut, tut, mock rock' . . . just cast it off in two words. I thought it was great though."

The frenetic pace continued as the Dolls made their way through London, where they had reservations in South Kensington at the splendid Blakes Hotel which David Jo described as "kinda deco and renovated looking". Further renovations would have to be carried out in the wake of the band's visit. Gathered in the hotel lobby to greet the Dolls was a welcoming party that included Malcolm McLaren and Vivienne Westwood who introduced the band to Ian Dury. A couple of members of Roxy Music mingled with a group of American girls who were keen to offer the Dolls some home grown fun. One of them, a tall chick with aspirations to be a musician called Chrissie Hynde, would pair off with Arthur.

The Dolls had a particularly busy schedule in front of them, starting with a soundcheck in the late afternoon at the Rainbow Room, a huge Art Deco lounge and bar on the sixth floor of Biba's department store in Kensington High Street. After the soundcheck, they were to return to Blakes for a press conference before getting ready for the Biba gig. The band drifted upstairs, where Frenchy began running a bath for Arthur. Sylvain: "We started hanging out with these American girls, and the bath was still running. We went to do the soundcheck, then me and Arthur went down to the department store. Arthur tried on a black jacket with a leopard collar which was priced at £40. Now although we were being treated like royalty we still didn't have any money, so Arthur switched the price tag on it for a £12 one. He wasn't shoplifting, switching tags was something Arthur and Billy had always done but the shop assistant figured it out and called for security. He was arrested and it made the local news that night."

Barbara Hulanicki, the creator of Biba, an opulent palace of purchases, had booked the Dolls for two nights. Indeed, they had the honour of being the first live band ever to strut their stuff in the Rainbow Room. Ms Hulanicki was most perturbed by the shoplifting incident, which she recounted in her biography *From – A – To Biba*: "The day they were due to appear we were watching their roadies setting up the equipment when the head of our security arrived, gripping two bedraggled looking creatures who had been caught shoplifting dresses and who claimed to work for us. They were part of the group and reluctantly we had to let them off. The Dolls did not go down very well with our audience either."

The chastened Dolls returned to Blakes, only to find that the hotel had been flooded by the bath that Frenchy had started running for Arthur which no one had bothered to turn off until soapy water started lapping around the shoes of surprised hotel guests. The press conference was delayed while the hotel management and the band's management held a screaming match in the foyer. David Jo went for Arthur when he found out who was responsible for the damage, and the press went for the band because they were tired of waiting.

The opening line of questioning was none too respectful but well fielded by Johansen . . .

"How much hose-pipe do you push down your trousers?"

"None. It's all me."

"Why are you trying to play down the outrage when before you played it up?"

"We never played it up, the Press did."

"Are any of you married, apart from to each other?"

"None of us are married."

"What kind of people do you expect to come and see you here, if anyone?"

"Decadents of all ages."

"Why are you playing Biba's?"

"Because we like playing in a cabaretish situation."

Every time the rest of the Dolls attempted to interject, Johansen hissed at them like an irate alley cat, until they sulkily retreated into simmering resentment. It had been a black day for Arthur but like the jacket with the leopard-skin collar he'd eventually managed to smuggle out of Biba's, it had a silver lining.

The Dolls' two consecutive shows at Biba's were a must-see for anyone who considered themselves movers in the rock, art or fashion world. Even Paul McCartney showed up. London tried to out-decadent New York but the lounge lizards and their sultry sirens were quite astonished at just how wild the Dolls were as they flailed about on stage in a maelstrom of raucous rock'n'roll. Sylvain: "They were expecting us to be the most incredible, major band. They weren't expecting dirty rootsiness from five little punky kids who had turned music upside down and started all over again."

The audience hadn't expected their ear drums to explode either. The band had borrowed the Rolling Stones' PA system via an associate of pianist Ian Stewart and while the system was perfect for a stadium, it sounded somewhat boomy in the confines of the Rainbow Room. Malcolm McLaren was utterly enraptured: "It was fantastic. They were like the worst strip-tease rock act you can imagine. I loved their awkward, trashy vibe. We became a part of their entourage and like groupies we followed them to Paris."

On November 28, The New York Dolls travelled to France. It

could have been turbulence or it might have been a champagne hangover from the forty bottles of bubbly that the band insisted Biba provide, but Thunders and Nolan felt so sick on the journey that for once neither of them were particularly into booze that day. Being a Doll wasn't a healthy option at the best of times but Johnny and Jerry's symptoms were a little different from the usual morning-after-the-night-before nausea. Peter Jordan: "I noticed that Johnny and Jerry were acting a little funny. That was the first time I became aware of their abuse of narcotics. When Jerry joined the Dolls he didn't even smoke cigarettes, he didn't do any kind of drugs, he didn't drink. If he did go out and have something to drink, it'd be something really corny like whisky and soda. It was a surprise to me that either of them had gotten into heroin. Johnny was a hip guy and he'd been around the block, even though he was very young. Frankly, there was enough aggravation already going on, so the last thing I expected anyone to do was get strung out on heroin."

The Dolls' arrival at Orly Airport became infamous, with Thunders taking over the late Billy Murcia's unfortunate predilection for public vomiting. Waiting alongside the gathering pack of press photographers at the airport was Patrick Taton, a dour French employee of Mercury Records who was supposed to look after the band during their visit but in private kept a damning dossier which he later submitted to the record company. Paul Nelson managed to liberate the confidential file which begins at Orly. "Thunders got sick right on the airport floor and had to leave the scene for a minute to pull himself together and make a decent comeback," wrote Taton.

Splattered with vomit, the photographers and reporters wiped themselves down and returned to their news desks to write reams of salacious prose and develop their pictures. Sylvain: "It was all over the press, The Dolls arrive in France and they are degenerate, drug-addicted faggots."

Only *NME*'s Nick Kent, no stranger to decadence having

studied chemical abuse in the court of The Rolling Stones, was able to inject a little humour into the scenario ... "Johnny Thunders throws up. Bl-a-a-a-a-g-g-h! God knows how many photographers are there: *Paris Match*, *Stern* magazine – all the European rock press and the nationals. The record company folks have arranged a special little welcome. Bl-a-a-a-a-g-g-h-h! The members of the band look stone-faced and wasted, wondering if he's maybe going to fall into his own vomit ..."

The Dolls eventually made it to their hotel, tailed by Taton, who noted: "The band gave us a hint as to their drinking capacities, which we had to discover at our own expense. In the afternoon, Thunders got sick again and had to be replaced by one of the road managers for photo purposes." When the Dolls played in Lyons that night, Patrick Taton did not share in the audience's enthusiasm, nor did he the following evening in Lille. Instead he waited for the band's Paris début, poison pen at the ready.

Les Poupees Du New York enjoyed a riotous first night in the French capitol. Their entourage now included Malcolm McLaren and his couturier friend Jean-Charles Castellbajac, who was celebrating his birthday. They all sat down to dinner at La Coupole, a chic brasserie in Montparnasse. Before the dessert arrived, the band's management wisely bailed out and returned to the hotel, conveniently assuming that McLaren would foot the bill. Malcolm McLaren: "I suppose their managers thought that us Europhiles had money to burn, being foolish entrepreneurial shopkeepers who were running around after the Dolls, but of course I couldn't pay the bill. It was a banquet for twenty people, including all these various hangers-on and because it was Jean-Charles' birthday, I'd ordered a huge cake. We had to run for it and these two young French journos got collared by the staff and slung back into the restaurant, where they had to find a way to pay the bill. We finally got back to the Ambassador Hotel, where the Dolls were staying and collapsed, exhausted from running all the way. I suppose that was my first real affair with the Dolls, my initiation into their lifestyle and I was attracted enough to continue."

The following day, at 12 o'clock sharp, Patrick Taton sat down in the bar of the Ambassador Hotel to take notes on the Dolls' press conference. Unsurprisingly, at that early hour, the band were nowhere to be seen. Marty Thau had been attempting to corral his unruly charges since nine o'clock that morning but had only managed to locate three of them. Meanwhile, the bar area was spilling over with reporters from Spain, Italy, Holland, Germany and France. To stave off any ill-feeling about the band's tardiness, Thau threw open the bar. Marty: "It was like a United Nations gathering of rock'n'roll writers. I knew the press conference was never going to take place at 12, so I told the writers to have a drink and wait for the band. By four o'clock there was an $8,000 bar tab which Mercury had to pay for and they weren't too happy about it. I got yelled at for it but we certainly got a lot more than $8,000 worth of press out of it."

By late afternoon all of the Dolls had assembled in the bar and the interviews got underway. As usual, David Johansen nursed a bottle of Remy Martin, his favourite accessory, as he entertained the gentlemen of the press. If Arthur was a withdrawn drunk, who could on occasion barely negotiate his way on stage, David Jo was a loud lush, capable of being either extremely witty or a mean-mouthed bitch, depending on circumstances. Sylvain: "Arthur and I used to call him Tu Tu Fly – he used to be like a drunk Bette Davis."

David handed out more scoops to the journalists than an inebriated waitress in an ice-cream parlour. "I've checked out all this 'Paris-is-the-city-of-romance' thing. It's just because all the chicks have to get it at least five times a day or else they go crazy," was among his more piquant observations.

The liquor loosened talk turned to the subject of the Dolls' projected second album, tentatively entitled *Too Much Too Soon*, and some of their newer compositions, which gave Thunders – not the most verbally forthcoming of characters –

a chance to talk about what he liked best, the music: "Well there's 'Mystery Girls' and, uh, one that I wrote called 'Jailbreak Opera'. It's short y'know – no longer than five minutes. I just like to grab everything ya can, throw it all in and get out, y'know." Johansen jumped right in where the guitarist paused: "Also there's 'Puss'n'Boots', which is quite sensational. It's about shoe fetishism or as Arthur observed, it's about 'the woofers in relationship to the woofee'. And then we have this ballad which isn't quite finalised yet, but it's the most beautiful song since The Drifters' 'On Broadway'."

As the journalists began to depart, Sylvain gave them all a parting shot with his toy cap-gun. Marty Thau was left to face the music with Patrick Taton, who had written more in his Dolls' dossier than most of the press had scribbled into their notebooks all afternoon. Taton: "When the interviews were over, I picked up the bill, which was incredibly high for so short a time. When I told Thau about it, he replied, with utmost contempt, 'Peanuts for a band like that' and continued with some of the most insulting remarks I've ever heard about a record company and its executives."

The next entry in Patrick Taton's confidential Mercury report was made only a couple of hours after the press conference: "Next was a live concert at Radio Luxembourg. Although they had been requested for rehearsals at 17.30, the group were not ready before 19.00 and went to the studio in a frightening state of drunkenness – one of the most nerve-shattering experiences of my 'business' life." The Radio Luxembourg show, which is now available on CD as either *Paris Burning* or *Paris Le Trash*, is a lewdly reeling affair with only Jerry's solidly anchored drumming keeping the band in shape. Sylvain: "If you listen to that recording you can hear what condition David was in. He was a drunken mess. His ego had gone completely overboard and he couldn't do no wrong in his own eyes. He was trying to talk in French and he was so out of it."

On December 2, The New York Dolls played a matinée

show at the prestigious Olympia Theatre, where the likes of Edith Piaf, Charles Aznavour and James Brown had previously graced the stage. Much to Patrick Taton's surprise, the band managed to haul their asses out of bed reasonably early, a triumph for the persistent Frenchy. It was left to their valet to rouse the band whenever there was something of particular importance on their agenda. Reliving his days as an army sergeant in a training camp, Frenchy would go into the Dolls' rooms blowing a police whistle in a military style wake up and get moving exercise. Frenchy would also blow his piercing whistle when procuring girls for the band from the audience. "Okay. You! And You! And You!," he'd yell as the eager conscripts formed an orderly queue.

Not only had they risen early but the Dolls had gone down to the capacious theatre and soundchecked without a hitch. The band took a liquid lunch, which had repercussions when they went on stage in front of a full house at 3.30 pm. Sylvain: "We looked absolutely beautiful. We'd just come from London where we'd raided Vivienne's shop and got the loveliest things which we were trading back and forth between us. We're on stage in the mid-afternoon and Arthur was wearing these big white aviator boots that kind of glowed in the dark and this kid in the front row put some LSD on the front of his boots. The whole band had been drinking a lot, and basically Johnny didn't go to the john before the show so we're on the third or fourth song, and he had to go. He said something to David and walked right off. That really pissed David off. How could anybody walk off when he was about to sing? I filled in and played some blues . . . 'Lone Star Queen', and the kids started clapping along, Jerry got into it, swinging on a beat and David started blowing the harp, so it wasn't that bad. Johnny came back, he'd taken a leak behind an amp but the gig ended with a spat between David and Johnny." In between the encores, Johansen and Thunders sniped back and forth at each other, bickering through their moment of triumph.

After the gig, the French representatives of Mercury Records, including the ever-present Patrick Taton, took the Dolls out to dinner. Naturally Taton, who had appointed himself as some kind of moral watchdog, found plenty to write about: "The band were then taken to a top restaurant. They invited their friends – over 50 people altogether – all of them lavishly drinking champagne and Cognac, making an incredible show of themselves, enraging patrons, and leaving us with a very nice bill."

The New York Dolls had become their own fictional image of how they dreamed life in a rock band would be, but they didn't understand that they were now part of an industry with its own rules and regulations. Arthur Kane: "We had a lot of fun and got to live the fantasy of what a teenager would imagine it would be like to be a young rock star. We lived that, we were that. We were fans that came of age and had their dream come true and that's what in the end made it so disastrous for us." As Paul Nelson later explained: "If the Dolls were difficult to work with at times, it was because they understood nothing of the music business and recording, seemed naïve or unable to learn about either, and were rarely encouraged to exhibit any kind of self-control regarding the bankbook or the clock."

December 3 dawned in a state of crisis and closed in calamity. The day began with the news that Marty Thau and Steve Leber had returned to New York, leaving the group without any funds. The Dolls asked for and received an advance to bail them out but then scurried back into their rooms with their Parisienne playmates when they should have been preparing for an appearance on French TV. For over three hours Patrick Taton handled a barrage of calls from an irate television producer, who eventually threatened to cancel the show and swore he would never again work with any of Mercury's acts. Once the Dolls emerged, it transpired that the road crew had been dawdling in their duties and were five hours behind schedule in setting up the equipment at the television studio. Finally the show was taped and the Dolls left in a stretch Mercedes for their next engagement, a gig at The Bataclan on the Rue Voltaire. At the gymnasium-like venue there waited a French film maker who was shooting the Dolls for a short documentary that also featured The Who. She very much hoped the band would live up to their reputation, as did the hyped up audience who snaked around the block waiting for the Bataclan to open. The Dolls entered the venue through the back door and were taken upstairs to the dressing room area. Sylvain: "Johnny called me over to look out of the window. He goes 'Look, The Beatles are here.' We looked down and there was a fucking pool of people, it looked like something out of *A Hard Day's Night.* Johnny loved that, it was really cool to see him enjoying that. Of course, I loved it too."

When the Dolls came to do their set, however, the stage was crawling with people. On Sylvain's side, there was a gathering of Dolls' fans, but where Thunders usually stood, most of the space was taken up with aggressive street punks. Peter Jordan: "For some reason all the bouncers in the Bataclan were either Samoan or Haitian and the whole audience was male. The audience started doing this thing were they all linked arms and began doing this kind of runaround dance, it was like an early form of moshing. They were all running around in circles, knocking each other over and yelling, 'Fuck you. Fuck you.' Although it was edited out in the film, the bouncers started bopping the guys in the audience on the head with sticks. I didn't see exactly what happened from where I was but somehow Johnny gets involved in it and somebody got smacked in the head. It was a typical punk rock show."

From Jordan's vantage point he was unable to see the mounting tension in Thunders' corner but Sylvain was casually monitoring the situation. Sylvain: "A couple of the guys in front of Johnny started to spit at him. Johnny, of course, spat right back, then it escalated from spitting to kicking and then they threw something at him, so he picked up the microphone stand, you know how they have a heavy round base, like a weight, and he threw it right in their faces. After that, this guy and all his buddies went for us and we had to run off. Of course everyone remembers that as, 'Wow, the Dolls start a riot' but it was bad. Somebody could have got killed. If they'd have caught up with Johnny, who was the first one to put down his guitar and split, I don't think they would have let him go."

The fifteen minutes' worth of Bataclan footage shot by the documentary maker has since become the unholy grail of Dolls' ephemera, but the lady responsible for the filming held on to the reel for over twenty years, periodically offering it for sale at a ludicrous price. In 1995, the US underground film maker Lech Kowalski claimed to have done a deal for the footage, which is to be included in a future documentary about Johnny Thunders.

On December 4, the Dolls packed their vanity cases and bade farewell to France. Imitating Napoleon, so he wouldn't have to shake hands with the band, Patrick Taton hurried the Dolls out of the Ambassador and off to the airport, where they had to catch a flight to Germany. Taton's relief was brief when he discovered that the band had landed him with room service charges of over $3,500, mainly for drinks and long distance phone calls. After writing a check to the Ambassador, Taton filed his last report on the Dolls: "If I may offer a personal opinion, The New York Dolls are one of the worst examples of untogetherness I have ever seen. Johansen is a very intelligent guy, Sylvain is really clever and nice, the others are quite kind in their own way; but put them together, add their managers (each of them doing his own thing), mix with alcohol, and shake, and you've got a careless, selfish, vicious and totally disorganised gang of New York hooligans – and I'm really sorry to say so. Despite all this, I believe we have managed to do good business." Mercury shot the messenger once he'd delivered the dossier, and Taton was never heard of again in the music business.

The Dolls' flying visit to Germany was ostensibly a press and pose exercise. They played 'Looking For A Kiss' live on *Musikladen*, one of Germany's leading rock programmes, which was filmed in Bremen in front of a studio audience. Sylvain: "It was a good performance. Even though things weren't all that chummy-chummy, we still performed well. That trip to Europe was probably the last time we really did all work together as one. Doing television is as boring as hell, especially when you've got to do a take over and over. It drives everybody crazy and you've got to look like, 'Wow, this is exciting.' It's a trick to master but the Dolls got really good at that because we did so much television, whether it was lip-syncing or performing live."

The following day the Dolls performed exclusively for the German press and Mercury executives in Salambo's Boudoir, the former premises of the Star club, in Hamburg. The legendary club where The Beatles had cut their teeth now specialised in live sex shows. Being rock'n'roll fans, the Dolls were thrilled at the prospect of treading the same stage as The Beatles, despite history having erased their traces with a parade of writhing bodies. The majority of the German journalists who attended the gig were too uptight to appreciate the band or even the club's pretty Vietnamese waitresses. A photograph of the Dolls taken in the entrance of Salambo's Boudoir was eventually used for the back cover of their second album. Leaning between the rough plastered walls of a hallway illuminated with red lighting and haloed by blood red velvet drapes, the Dolls look like hostesses at the gateway to hell, as if something has died in their souls. Sylvain does a cheesy little bump'n'grind, Arthur looks weary and washed out, Jerry, hands on hips, appears ready to roll someone, and Johnny Thunders looks pinched, with shadows for eyes. Only Johansen, staring unflinchingly at the camera, shows any real signs of life.

The next stop on the Dolls' European itinerary was The Netherlands, where the band was booked to play 'Jet Boy' on *Avro's Top Pop*, a mainstream rock programme. Roxy Music were featured on the same show. A great b&w performance shot of the Dolls on the surreal set, with Johnny playing a white Vox Teardrop guitar that Arthur picked up in a Leeds pawn shop for £20, would soon grace a limited edition inner sleeve of *Too Much Too Soon* which for reasons unexplained was available only in the USA and France. This was followed by a gig at an Amsterdam university, at which the Dolls ran into trouble with a politically militant group called The Provos. Peter Jordan: "This was another of those shows where I pretended I had nothing to do with the band. The Dolls had never been politically inclined and we'd never been manipulated into taking a political stance like The MC5. We were pretty apolitical and asexual. There was a tremendous contingent of these militant, extremely left-wing Provos at the gig, and they started disrupting the show. I figured that because they had long hair, they were going to be into rock'n'roll but no, these pricks wanted to engage the band in some kind of dialogue. First off we were American, that was bad enough. They also took offence because we might be homosexual and they thought that the Dolls were taking the Mickey out of the hippie movement. The Provos got rowdy but nobody got hit or hurt. I mean they were a bunch of tubby wimps but after the show, they started rocking the tour bus."

On December 10, the Dolls made a fleeting trip to Brussels for yet another television appearance before returning to the States. Though relations between the band members were fraying, and Marty Thau and Steve Leber didn't always see eye to eye on certain issues anymore, and Mercury had begun to have serious misgivings about the band, at least this time none of the Dolls had to be sent back from Europe in a metal casket.

The New York Dolls finished off the year by touring the US, coming home to roost for Christmas. Johnny and Sabel moved into an apartment on West 24th Street which was furnished courtesy of Ma Genzale. Miss Starr, a total California girl, was finding New York tough. She'd all but starved while her man was away. If Alice Cooper's girlfriend Cindy Lang hadn't taken her out for dinner at Max's on a regular basis, Sabel might have slipped through the cracks in the sidewalk, leaving behind only a pair of high-heeled wedgies for posterity. New York's harsh climate also came as a shock. Sabel: "I was raised in Southern California. I had never been out in snow before. It was the coldest winter of my life. I freezed my ass off and you can't wear sandals in the snow. It was our very first Christmas together. Johnny was so sweet. He went out and bought me a red setter puppy and he took me to Central Park for a buggy ride."

For a brief period, Johnny and Sabel played the cosy couple. Heroin was not yet Thunders' main drug of choice and although he dabbled, he hadn't even brushed the notion of a habit. In fact, Johnny was still rather partial to heroin's opposite number on the narcotic spectrum – speed. Eliot Kidd, a musician friend of the Dolls who fronted The Demons and often jammed with Thunders after their respective bands finished rehearsing for the day, became attuned to both Thunder and Nolan's chemical tendencies. Eliot: "Once in a while Johnny would take me to have dinner at his mother's house. After dinner we'd go down in the basement and shoot speed. He didn't use needles then, he didn't know how to use them himself, so I used to have to do it for him."

After Billy Murcia's death, Johnny and Syl became inseparable, united by grief, but as Jerry Nolan eased himself into the band, the best buddy balance began to shift. Thunders was impressed by Nolan's know-how and streetwise sensibilities. Jerry Nolan: "I don't know why I could see through Johnny but I did, maybe it was the neighbourhood I grew up in. Why do you think we stayed together? It wasn't Syl, it wasn't Arthur, it wasn't David. It was me. There's a reason for that. I taught Johnny everything. Johnny got the blame for it all but I actually did it all. I'd been playing for 10 years before Johnny even got started and I knew all the dirty tricks."

Nolan had the ability to make Johnny tow the line, and was cool enough and tough enough to handle the diminutive firebrand. Jerry: "Johnny constantly tried to see what he could

116

get away with. First time we went on tour we got into a big fist fight in the back of a limousine. I kicked the shit out of him. Ever since that day, he was like my son, he loved me for it." Gradually Johnny and Jerry became the Dolls' version of Bonnie and Clyde. Wherever Nolan went, Thunders was sure to follow. At that point, Jerry Nolan was just chipping away at heroin, no big deal. It wasn't like he was the man with the golden arm or anything. Eliot Kidd: "Jerry was the only one that did heroin and I know 'cos I did it. We had a secret wink between us. Back then you locked all the doors, pulled the blinds down and went into the bathroom, it was the last taboo in drugs. It wasn't until years later, during punk, that people openly started doing heroin. Jerry was pretty together during the Dolls, I don't think he was doing heroin every day but he was doing it on a regular basis."

1973 was drawing to a close but The New York Dolls still had time to back off from the brink. Unfortunately, the volatile factors that made them one of the greatest rock'n'roll bands in history didn't allow for moderation or calm debate. Mercury was running out of patience with them and their only chance of redemption lay in a successful second album. The Dolls' début LP had fared well but Mercury were digging for gold. Marty Thau: "Mercury didn't think the Dolls were doing well because they'd only sold 110,000 copies of the first album. I was disappointed that it didn't get to number one but I concluded that it was a good start, all things considered. When Mercury told me we had only sold 110,000 copies, I said, 'Well what did you expect it to sell?' 'We thought we'd go gold with it,' they said. 'How many other acts do you have on your roster that sell 110,000 copies, the first time around?' I asked. They couldn't answer that. I realised that the tremendous press coverage the band got was in a sense working against them, because people expected them to accomplish the impossible."

The Dolls played the Allen Theater in Cleveland, Ohio on December 30, and brought in the New Year at the Michigan Palace, Detroit. From the stage, Johansen roared, "It's 74 – Open the door!" to a revved up 5,000 strong crowd. The gig was broadcast live on a local station WABX, and scorched the ears of all the stay-at-home listeners. Opening with 'Personality Crisis', 'Bad Girl' and 'Looking For A Kiss', the band were at their strident best. A thunderous version of 'Who Are The Mystery Girls' galloped into 'Stranded In The Jungle', Johansen bellowing like King Kong and Sylvain making with the monkey noises.

If there were conflicts in the Dolls' camp it didn't show on stage that night. 'Human Being', 'Pills' and 'Trash' were delivered in a rapid-fire burst before David Jo handed over the centre stage to Johnny T. The lead guitarist had fought for and finally won a spot in the Dolls' set he could call his own. While Johansen skipped around with a tambourine, Johnny shredded the riffs of his solo composition 'The Milk Man'. The saga of a foot fetishist known as 'Puss'n'Boots' was next. Somehow the Dolls could tack together a mess of a tune and make it fabulous.

That night, the denizens of Detroit got the keys to Babylon from Johansen: "This one's about our home town but when we were writing it, we didn't know that Detroit was the murder capitol of the United States so we're going to dedicate this one to you kids tonight . . . Babylon!" The Dolls' answer to 'New York New York' is no place for tourists: "I was driving round drunk boys/And I was gone/The cops asked me where do I come from/One looked at my cards/Where's my I.D.?/When you can tell by my face/It's so easy to see/I'm from Babylon". The location changes for 'Lone Star Queen', a shlocky R&B brawl with Johansen exhorting the band to 'V-i-b-e-r-a-t-e!'

Once they'd finished 'V-i-b-e-r-a-t-i-n-g' and got through the encores, the band collapsed backstage. Sylvain: "We were massive in Detroit. We had that street sound that really appealed to those kids who were waiting for a change. Everybody would come to those shows all dressed up. I remember New Year's Eve in Detroit, our road manager counting out the $14,000 we made that night. That was a lot of money, then."

The Dolls' house was in need of a little scaffolding but it wasn't yet ready to be condemned.

8

Lipstick Killers & Dolls' Molls

They were the kind of girls who never took off their make-up before going to bed. They hung out with bikers in black leather and boys in street gangs. At their earliest shows they stripped down to their garter belts, a ploy to pad out a set with hardly any material in it. They were arrested 16 times during their short career and even convicted of gun-running. Along with their producer and mentor, George 'Shadow' Morton, The Shangri-Las gave voice to all the sad, bad girls that the other girl groups of the time wouldn't have dared represent. Tragedy, a sense of drama in every inflection, unhappy love affairs, motel rooms instead of honeymoon suites, all were enhanced by Shadow Morton with an orchestra of effects. He didn't so much produce as provide a B-movie soundtrack for The Shangri-Las' four top twenty hits. Between September 1964 and November 1965, the girls peaked with 'Remember (Walking In The Sand)', 'Leader Of The Pack', 'Give Him A Great Big Kiss' and 'I Can Never Go Home Anymore'. By 1966, they had pretty much gone the way of their songs, back out into the streets. The personnel, originally two sets of sisters, began to change. None of them made any money. One Shangri-La went to heaven and no doubt the others drifted into unhappy marriages.

The Shangri-Las were The New York Dolls' soul sisters, and with this in mind Marty Thau set out to find the whereabouts of Shadow Morton with a view to asking him to produce the Dolls' second album. Unfortunately for the Dolls, Shadow hadn't been sealed in a time capsule since 1965 and the man who wrote 'Leader Of The Pack' and 'Give Him A Great Big

Kiss' was older and weirder. Paul Nelson: "Shadow Morton . . . talk about a mysterious man. There was no way to contact Shadow by phone ever, except at this little bar. He reeked of Monty Clift and James Dean and he had this philosophical religious thing. He'd go on forever about this Pan religion stuff. It didn't make much sense but it was fascinating."

In between The Shangri-Las and the Dolls, Shadow had worked with Vanilla Fudge and Janis Ian before dropping out to pursue a high velocity interest in racing cars. He narrowly avoided the kind of death crash scenario The Shangri-Las sang about, recovered from paralysis and waited for fortune to smile again. Morton hadn't heard of the Dolls and presumed they were some kind of a girl group until he was invited by Thau to watch them rehearse at the Media Sound Studio on West 57th Street. After a further meeting, Morton agreed to a $10,000 production fee, just enough to buy a Winnebago and live out his retirement dream of travelling around the United States.

Shadow's appointment was far from a democratic decision. Sylvain: "Shadow Morton was never my pick. He'd been groovy in the Sixties but compared to what we were doing, it was like night and day. We had a list of possible producers to choose from. Todd Rundgren's name was on there again, and Bob Ezrin. Shadow was added later as a novelty suggestion but of course David hit the roof when he heard his name. Johnny wasn't really making the right decisions, he wasn't really all there and he'd got his big concession to sing one song. The thing is, we walked out of that meeting with Shadow as one of several possibilities, then Marty hunted him down."

On January 28, Morton and The New York Dolls entered A&R Studios to begin work on *Too Much Too Soon*. Taking the name of their second album from actress Diana Barrymore's autobiography which was later filmed under the same title, the Dolls played into the hands of fate. Too many tragic heroines can drag a boy under, and Barrymore was a classic. Born into the famed Barrymore acting dynasty, whose performances on and off stage made the Hollywood headlines of the Thirties and Forties and continues today with Drew Barrymore, Diana's life was a riches to rags story propelled by liquor, pills and suicide attempts. "I swallowed the pills and washed them down with whisky, then swallowed the rest and washed them down too. Damn I thought. I won't be able to read my obituary. Who will be at my funeral, I wonder," she wrote in *Too Much Too Soon*. According to an interview with David Jo in *Circus* magazine, it wasn't suicide that finally offed Diana Barrymore but an irate partner who rammed a tennis ball down her throat. Johansen: "*Too Much Too Soon* is a eulogy to Diana Barrymore . . . she had a foul life anyway."

As Johansen and Thunders, the band's main songwriting team, were now increasingly estranged from one another, there was very little new material for the album. 'Babylon', the opening track, could hardly be considered a fresh offering but it's still a great journey home to modern day Sodom and Gomorrah, with its images of go-go dancers and massage parlours, spurred along by a grinding bass and fractured guitars. Prior to the Dolls going into the studio with Shadow Morton, they demoed, amongst other material, two of Sylvain's compositions, 'Teenage News' and 'Too Much Too Soon'. A dreamy, hypnotic song, Johnny T would later make use of 'Too Much Too Soon' during his solo career. To Sylvain's dismay, the potential title track was not even considered for the album, even though four cover versions – 'Stranded In The Jungle', '(There's Gonna Be A) Showdown', 'Bad Detective' and 'Don't Start Me Talking' – appeared on it. Sylvain: "I went to talk to Shadow Morton and asked him what was going to happen but he was in a hurry. He was too quick with me and said that he'd been told only to listen to David Johansen and Johnny Thunders. He didn't want to tell me who had told him that but obviously it was the managers. I just walked out, it was all driving me nuts."

'Stranded In The Jungle', a once proud number when handled live by the Dolls, is toned down by Morton's middle of

the road production from a crazy hot-house boogaloo with a
Cab Calloway influence into a cabaret turn. Whatever sparks of
inspiration Shadow had once run on, he was now misfiring on
all cylinders. Morton, in print at least, appeared to like the
band and told Lenny Kaye in an article for *Melody Maker*:
"They're dealing in strict conviction, of breaking the mould.
They're dealing in the reality that there are no barriers, old
barriers should be torn down and you should go to whatever
extreme you have to. I love that. They get me off; I hope I get
them off."

Why then did Shadow, who liked to read Tibetan philosophy
in the studio, attempt to make the Dolls sound like a conventional supper-club blues band? It's only because of The
New York Dolls' untameable wildness that the material on the
album managed to retain any character. While the band were
spitting, Morton was polishing. 'Who Are The Mystery Girls?'
caters well to Johansen's vocals but keeps a controlling leash
on the normally painful guitar runs. It was no secret that the
Dolls were in need of a hit single and their current producer
wanted to see them attain it but perhaps the only way the Dolls
could have topped the single charts back then was through
group castration. The studio take of '(There's Gonna Be A)
Showdown', which the band usually turned to when rioting
broke out at their gigs, wouldn't have quelled an uprising by
two-year-olds but it is fun. Side one of *Too Much Too Soon* draws
to a close with the sublime 'It's Too Late' which David Jo once
described as 'a little abstract expressionism'. Dating back to
the Chrystie Street loft days and dedicated to Diana Dors,
'It's Too Late' shakes a tail feather at all the jaded, faded
Hollywood Babylonians who can't 'Parlez New York Francais'.
Sylvain's steady strumming leaves room for some shuddering
guitar licks from Thunders, while Johansen plays the cynical
ingenue . . . "Well you invite us up to that space trip/Well that
was nothing new on me/It reminds me of Buck Rogers back in
1933".

Lenny Kaye reported on the progress of *Too Much Too Soon*

for *Melody Maker*: "The last album was recorded in eight days, but they're taking more time with this one, bringing in occasional strings and horns, following Shadow's advice not 'to settle'. David Jo Hansen likes his new producer, thinks he has an ear for what's happening, appreciates the 'looser' feel that's coming over their music. 'That man is completely unpretentious,' he tells me between sidelong glances at Lesley Gore on an alcove television showing the TAMI show. 'He doesn't think he ever did a marvellous thing in his life.' Lesley Gore accepts the plaudits of the crowd and scampers off. David slips out to do a take with the band on 'It's Too Late'. Shadow stretches to the microphone, lets them know it's 'lucky seven comin' atcha', then rocks back in his swivel chair, dice hands clasped, a proud poppa on the way to a brand new pair of shoes. Later, Arthur comes lumbering out of the studio. 'You know,' he says in that *Exorcist*-whispered voice, looking a little dazed, 'I actually feel like a serious musician this time around.' "

'Puss'n'Boots', the album's only Johansen/Sylvain collaboration, kicks off the second side of *Too Much Too Soon*. Taking its name from a podoerotic quarterly available in adult book stores that contains illustrated articles with such tempting titles as 'To Stomp A Dude', 'Bitches In Boots' and 'They Suck Shoes Don't They?', the song deals with the trials of 'Little Rhinestone Target' who has to change his name in order to pursue his fetish. Unfortunately he gets shot in the attempt . . . "Don't you know the boots are making him lame?" Arthur's bass playing bounces like a rickshaw on cobblestones, accompanied by the macho tread of Nolan's drums. The brassy vocals are cornered in a treacherous crossfire of guitars until 'Puss'n'Boots' is finally silenced by a gunshot stolen from The Olympic's track 'Western Movies'.

Although Johnny Thunders' 'Jailbreak Opera' never materialised, 'Chatterbox' a.k.a. 'The Milk Man' a.k.a. 'Milk Me' made its vinyl début. With roots planted long ago in Billy's basement, 'Chatterbox' marks out Thunders' hard won territory. The

tough little no-nonsense rocker which led David Jo to con-
cede that Thunders had "a cute voice", concerns a crossed-wire
phone connection ... "Say Chatterbox/I said you squawk a
lot/C'mon gimme some lips". If lyric writing wasn't always
Thunders' greatest talent, his guitar playing spoke volumes and
his reply to Miss Chatterbox is a highly strung evocation of
accelerating frustration.

The former Coasters' number 'Bad Detective' takes the
Dolls' on a fast boat to China for a Charlie Chan mystery.
Adorned by the daftest ever backing vocals, 'Bad Detective'
leaves the Dolls sounding like a drunk-on-sake chorus line of
geisha girls. The track is a raucous mix of oriental hokum
leading to a chop suey climax with Mr Chan ... "So we're
trapped up in a warehouse/Much to our surprise/Five big
machine guns/Staring in our eyes" ... While the Dolls' rendition of 'Bad Detective' is a fantastic pantomime, its inclusion
alongside the other covers on the album gave certain critics
the excuse to label the band as a novelty act. Two long established staples of the Dolls' live shows, 'Don't Start Me Talking'
and 'Human Being', bring the album to a screeching halt. To
all those who considered the Dolls to be unseemly trollops
'Human Being' could be construed as something of a plea.
David told *Circus* magazine: "We don't want our fans to think
we're weird or anything."

In the meantime, a bluesy little advert complete with some
soulful harmonica and end-of-the-night piano tinkling was
broadcast on a local NY radio station to promote the Dolls'
forthcoming gig at the Academy Of Music. In his smoky,
saloon-bar voice, Johansen announced ... "Babe, I'm getting
tired of this, seeing your face every night through the winter.
There's one thing, tho', one thing about this winter. We got
The New York Dolls coming to the Academy Of Music on
Friday night, February 15. We got our own St Valentine's Day
Massacre, honey ..." The gig was one of the Dolls' last great
gestures. Dispensing with the usual pink and cutesy Valentines

tricks, the band decided to paint the town blood red and turn gangster as The Lipstick Killers.

With the aid of Bob Gruen, a story line was developed around The Lipstick Killers – featuring 'Giovanni' Genzale, 'Rocky' Johansen, 'Killer' Kane, 'Scarface' Nolan and Sylvain as 'Legs' – the gang who couldn't do a job without their lipstick on. Bob Gruen: "We decided we'd make a newsreel of them as Thirties type gangsters as part of the Academy of Music show. The film ends with them riding up 14th Street firing off machine guns, then running into the theatre. Then they would suddenly appear for real, running down the aisles wearing the same gangster costumes, shooting the audience. Now for some people in the audience who were on the right drugs and peaking at the right time, this worked amazingly well. I know some people for whom this was the experience of a lifetime! There was this one kid who got beaten up by the guards because he got so hysterically excited."

Filmed in one day and edited in three weeks 'Lipstick Killers' is a delicious B&W spoof, spliced between genuine old news footage, that follows the gang as they evade the Feds in a metro manhunt. Bob Gruen: "We got a guy to film them in a whole bunch of different gangster settings. They were great actors, they would really get into a role and be spot on and they were funny. There's this one scene where they're putting on lipstick and each guy applies it in his own unique style, like Johnny, one swipe and he's done. Arthur has to hold the thing with two hands 'cos he's shaking so bad. David does it with flair and gets it right. We bought some old Movietone news reels and out of it we chose to use some footage of a Twenties beauty contest with these women posing in outrageously ugly bathing suits. We found a great scene of Babe Ruth in Hollywood where a woman's putting make-up on him and a clip of a prison riot. The newsreel opens with Hitler surrounded by little boys and he's patting them on the head, then there's the German invasion of France. Suddenly there's a news flash with the Dolls marching up the street shooting into the camera, to make the audience aware that this was a trailer for the band and not just some weird film."

In a stern voice-over, citizens are warned to be careful for there is no telling where the Lipstick Killers will strike again. Nobody, not even Elliot Ness, could have saved the audience at the Academy of Music, who had sat patiently through the support acts. Elliot Murphy, a blond singer with *Great Gatsby* pretensions did a turn before Kiss, who had just signed to Neil Bogart's Casablanca Records. Bob Gruen: "Kiss told me they were inspired by the Dolls. They'd gone to see them play at the Diplomat Hotel and thought they were fantastic plus they loved it that there where all these girls at the gig. They said that at their next rehearsal they'd had a meeting about what they were going to look like and decided that they couldn't compete with the Dolls because they were gorgeous so they would go the opposite way and become monsters." With the entrepreneur Neil Bogart and a tight management team behind them, Kiss would be the first of many successful groups that followed in the Dolls' shaky footsteps, and like so many others they would be steered dear of the obstacles that tripped up the Lipstick Killers.

Nick Kent had been dispatched to New York to report on the local rock scene for London's *New Musical Express*, and he managed to catch the Dolls' performance at The Academy. "Their (the Dolls') popularity has reached such proportions in their home town that the only way it appears one can get laid in New York these days is to be part of their entourage," he wrote. "Their concert at the Academy of Music was easily the best I attended throughout my thoroughly depressing stay in the city. The fact alone that numerous male members of the audience had organised their whole visual around whichever member of the Dolls was their fave-rave (which meant numerous Johnny Thunders bouffant shag-cuts and Harpo Marx curls *à la* Sylvain Sylvain) is proof positive that there is some kind of life-blood pumping away in New York rock. Also, the Dolls had improved immeasurably, sounding, dare one say, almost professional and the new numbers like 'Puss'n'Boots' and 'Chatterbox' are gems, fulfilling a function for the Seventies in exactly the same way that numbers like 'Substitute' and 'Pictures Of Lily' did for the Sixties."

Immediately after the Dolls' Valentine spectacular, the band went back on the road in the run-up to the release of *Too Much Too Soon*. February 16 saw them in Bloomington, Indiana, with support from Lynyrd Skynyrd, followed by a gig in Cambridge, Massachusetts. They detoured back to Passaic, New Jersey, for a date at the Capitol Theatre where Steve Leber was waiting for them with some friendly advice. Arthur Kane: "We were doing the soundcheck when our managers walked in and said: 'This is Tom O'Horrigan, the famous Broadway choreographer, he's going to take a look at what you guys are doing'. We all looked at each other, like, 'Oh brother!' Out of everyone in the group, he picked me out and said, 'Okay, you over there, stand on this block.' So he stands me on this little pedestal, which is one square foot round. The fact of the matter is I was always drinking and stumbling around and I was wearing platform boots, so he picked the least likely character to put on a pedestal and tell me to stay there. I told him it was crazy and I wasn't going to do it. He hit the ceiling and stormed out of the theatre. It was so absurd for our managers to have sent in a choreographer." That night, the gig at the Capitol Theatre was disrupted but it wasn't by the Dolls attempting to perform a choreographed version of 'Puss'n'Boots'n'Swan Lake', rather a gaggle of nude dudes stormed the stage, leaving Johansen to proclaim the event a 'Streaker's Festival'.

With a March 16 gig at the Santa Monica Civic Center in LA fast approaching, Sabel Starr accompanied the band *en route* to her home town. When the Dolls hit Vancouver and Seattle, Miss Starr was gratified to discover that she was now a profile rock'n'roll girlfriend whose risqué reputation was recognised even beyond NY and LA, and it wasn't just the boys in the band who got asked for their autographs. To their fans,

Johnny Thunders and Sabel Starr had become imbued with a damaged glamour, the Seventies answer to Keith Richards and Anita Pallenberg. As an 'official' Doll's moll, Cyrinda Foxe was also getting her fair share of attention and, much like her partner, she exuded a strong and sassy persona, with no hint of the fragility that afflicted Thunders and Starr. *Rock Scene* magazine frequently featured photo spreads of David Jo and Cyrinda, giving them the status of a home grown Mick and Marianne, but with a much more playful edge. Cyrinda: "It was really fun, kids from all over the country would buy *Rock Scene* to see what was happening in New York, in the same way that we'd loved seeing pictures of what was happening in London. We'd get photographed for *Rock Scene* doing these funny things . . . 'Cyrinda Goes To The Hairdressers', 'Cyrinda And David Have A Barbecue On The Fire Escape', 'Cyrinda And David Go Shopping'."

The Dolls wouldn't have returned to LA before the release of their second album had it not been for the animator Ralph Bashki. Best known for his feature length pornographic cartoon film *Fritz The Cat*, Bashki adored the Dolls and wanted to include them in his latest animated venture *Hey Good Looking*. Peter Jordan: "The movie takes place in the Fifties and the Dolls somehow get transported in a time warp and wind up playing a High School prom. The only thing I remember about it is that I got repeated calls from the prop department that somebody, specifically Johnny and Syl, had stolen switchblades, leather jackets and various other things." Although the Dolls were filmed for *Hey Good Looking* under the premise that the animation would later be fitted around them, Ralph Bashki ran into financial trouble with his backers. The film was put on hold and when it was eventually released by another company, the Dolls were cut out of the story.

Ever since the impact of 'Lipstick Killers' on the audience at the Academy Of Music, other venues had been requesting that the short film be shown before the band went on stage. At first Bob Gruen was nonplussed, assuming that it wouldn't work out of context. The Dolls' gig at the Santa Monica Civic Center changed his mind. Bob Gruen: "I was there when they showed the film and people loved it, they all applauded, then the band came out and played the show. It had nothing to do with running down the aisles or the plot of the gig and I just couldn't understand it. After the show I was talking to Sabel Starr and I asked her about it. She was saying, 'Oh the film is great, the Dolls are movie stars!' I said: 'Yeah but we made the film specifically for the Academy show, it makes no sense when it's shown at other gigs.' Sabel goes: 'If you're in a movie, you're a star.' "

Miss Starr glowed with pride as she left the Santa Monica Civic Center, arm in arm with her matinee idol, little realising that her honeymoon with Thunders was just about to lose its candy coating. Sabel: "The day after the gig my parents came to the Beverly Hills Hotel and met Johnny. They were pretty impressed, the Dolls were starting to get famous. Then we went to a big party in a club, Iggy was there with Corel, all my friends were there, when Johnny dragged me into the bathroom. He thought I'd been flirting with Arthur, Arthur Kane *of all people*. He smacked my head so hard against the wall it broke a mirror. I just freaked. My head was bleeding, I had a big gash in it. Corel was going, 'What's going on?' I said, 'I don't know.' That was the first time he hit me. It was the beginning of the torture and the nightmare for me."

Following gigs in San Diego and Providence, Rhode Island, the Dolls returned to New York where a week's worth of dates in Manhattan awaited them. Advertised as their world tour, it was a cute move but for the most part it took them back to the small clubs where they'd launched their career, and masked the fact that some of the bigger promoters were turning their backs on the band. The influential Howard Stein, who had put the Dolls on at The Waldorf Astoria, excommunicated the band after the Halloween show. In part this was down to the audience's petty vandalism and high spirits but the Dolls themselves were becoming increasingly unstable and ridiculously unpunctual. Bob Gruen: "The Dolls' shows were so much fun, they would over-sell and there would be all these drunken, stoned people breaking the seats, and trying to smash down the doors to get in, there would be general havoc at whatever place the Dolls were playing. As they got more and more popular it got harder for them to find places to book them. They also got more and more late for gigs, not that they wouldn't show up, but as they got later they got drunker. Drugs also became more a part of the scene. I saw several shows where dealers would show up and Johnny and Jerry would just be nodding on stage, staring at the wall. Backstage, they were more remote and it was less fun to be around them as they got downed out."

The first date of the Manhattan world tour, on Sunday April 14 at My Father's Place on Long Island, was pitched as an Easter treat. Broadcast live on WBAB, the set opened with a sluggish, heavy rendition of 'Babylon' but like Mohammed Ali bouncing back from the ropes, the rest of the performance is a lightning bout with some typically witty repartee. Johansen tells the audience: "Y' know, my mother thinks I'm a real hard boiled egg" only for Sylvain to drolly retort, "She's right." 'It's Too Late' momentarily loses its bearings before getting back to full speed and a down and dirty cover of Willie Dixon's 'Hoochie Coochie Man' is a slow burning highlight. April 15 and 16 saw the Dolls playing back at Max's Kansas City but the big date on their mini-world tour was a drag show at the 82 Club on April 17.

Located off 2nd Avenue at 82 East 4th Street, the 82 Club had been an influential drag venue since its opening in 1953. Anyone who wanted to make it as a serious drag artist performed there and by the mid-sixties it was a big draw for any celebrities who wanted to take a little walk on the wig side. By the following decade however, the club had lost its clandestine appeal and most of its clientele. The Stonewall riots had taken drag out of secretive smoky bars and on to the street. David Jo: "We used to always go there and say to Tommy, who was this butch dyke who took the tickets, 'You should have rock'n'roll here'. The place was dying, that whole speakeasy element was over 'cos everything was out in the open. People didn't have to go there and hide what they were doing any more but Tommy didn't get it. 'Where are all the people going?' 'They're doing it in the street, Tommy.' "

The Dolls brought rock'n'roll to the 82 Club and in keeping with its policy that all gender should be subverted, Cyrinda Foxe wore a suit while her boyfriend borrowed one of her dresses. Cyrinda: "David wore my low cut red and white sequinned dress. Johnny wouldn't wear a dress, he just wouldn't do it and I thought he was the only hip one there. Sylvain wore chaps with his ass hanging out which was okay. Now, Arthur could get away with wearing a dress and not look like a fag, he looked like the precursor of all those boys who wear combat boots but with big dresses and dreadlocks but David looked like a flaming queen. He came off as a flaming queen. In fact, who knows? You hear stories . . ." Jerry Nolan, who having cut his hair just past his shoulders and greased it back was little by little regaining his masculinity, once again had to give up any leanings towards his natural state of dandified machismo and showed up for the gig wearing a demure polka dot dress with a velvet trim.

The Dolls' audience also entered into the spirit of the occasion and the gig was delayed, not by any of their usual antics but simply because of a surge of photographers taking pictures of anything in high heels, which was everyone except the ladies. David Jo: "The stage was behind the bar, so when you're singing, the bartender is in front of you. Butchie the bartender was Tommy's partner and she had one of those voice box things that you hold up to your neck to talk. We used to really like Butchie, she was really something. We played the first song and Butchie's trying to get my attention from the bar, waving her hands at me and kicking me on the leg, so I lean over 'cos I can't hear her because of the voice box, which she then puts up to her neck and says, 'I always thought you were a fag.' "

There followed two midnight shows at the Coventry in Queens on April 19 and 20, but the penultimate gig on the Dolls' miniature world odyssey was brought to a shattering finale by Arthur Kane. Eliot Kidd: "They played the Bottom Line and Arthur was really drunk after the show. In the dressing room, the walls were mirrored and Arthur picked up a bottle of booze and threw it at the wall. The whole thing cracked. He just turned around and split and the only people that were left in there was David, Frenchy and me. These two seven foot bouncers, who were so big their shadows filled up the doorway, came in wanting to know who broke the mirror. I was thinking, 'I'm not even in this band and I'm going to die tonight.' David looks at me and goes, 'Well, I'll fight if you'll fight' when Marty Thau appears and offers to pay for the damage." They quite literally blew out the last show on their week-long itinerary at Kenny's Castaways. For a band who liked to kick in brand new amplifiers to produce a cracked effect, and played so loud they transcended distortion, the club's sound system proved too puny and broke down during the Dolls' set.

In May 1974, The New York Dolls achieved the supreme accolade of being voted by *Creem* magazine as both the best and worst group of the year. On the downside, the Dolls were considered to be even more dreadful than The Osmonds, Grand Funk Railroad, Slade and Dawn. However the Dolls beat Queen, Aerosmith and Lynyrd Skynyrd for the number one slot at the top. A similar sense of confusion prevailed when *Too Much Too Soon* was released on May 10. Ron Ross, writing a favourable review for *Phonograph Record* attempted to place the album beyond the Dolls' devoted fan base ... "It's hard to predict, finally, who the Dolls' audience will be when all is said and done. The disco element is far more into Love Unlimited than glam or popcorn, and rightly so, since Barry White has brought the girl group into the Seventies without any sense of humour at all to get in your way when you're cruising. The pop boy and girl on the street are too concerned with looking like what the Dolls have enabled them to look like to listen very well to what the Dolls are actually doing. Too many kids are addicted to 'what's happening' to laugh at it, so it appears certain and probably best that the Dolls have gone beyond their initial scene orientation. An attempt to attract listeners who have nothing to do really with the boys' much discussed and seldom understood lifestyle, *Too Much Too Soon* is the first album the Dolls have made since they became public property, and while the album may not be a self-important manifestation of ultimate anything, it's no poke in the eye with a mascara wand either."

One thing was certain, however. Aside from a bevy of ever loving stalwarts, The New York Dolls were losing their grip as press darlings. The whip hand on the backlash was waiting to come down hard. *Circus* magazine lambasted the album . . . "The new LP is another wall of noise, cut after cut of annoying screeching, with David's feeble voice drowned out of each cut." In an attempt to be cruel to be kind, *NME*'s Nick Kent issued a stern warning . . . "The overall impression though is that this album is messy and shot through with unfulfilled potential. It's exactly the wrong sort of product to launch on a public, liberally weighed out with folk only too ready to pull the whole 'I told you so' number at the Dolls' expense. Too much, too soon with too little as the end result is bad multiplication and bad business. Get wise, guys!"

Little Steven Morrissey, who still hadn't recovered from seeing the Dolls on *The Old Grey Whistle Test*, and had been petitioning Laura Kauffmann, a pleasant employee at Mercury Records, for permission to start up a UK Dolls' fan club ever since, received a long awaited reply from Miss Kauffmann, in which mention is made of Kent's review . . . "We saw that Nick Kent review in *NME* and were quite upset by it as he had spent some time with the Dolls in the studio and had gone to see their concerts here when they played for a week in the little NY clubs where they first started. We were most upset when we figured out that he couldn't possibly have heard a finished product in time for the review to be written which is really quite unfair to the band."

Laura Kauffmann's ongoing support for the Dolls was something of a rarity at Mercury Records, and her loyalty would eventually get her a job at Leber and Krebbs' management company. Paul Nelson had been unofficially frozen out by Mercury and could no longer mediate on behalf of the Dolls. Nelson: "After the Dolls signed, I lasted another year and a half at Mercury but I wasn't trusted at all. I don't think I signed another band. I was still present at Mercury but whatever I said didn't mean anything to anybody anymore."

When *Too Much Too Soon* got off to an even shakier start than the Dolls' début album had done, Mercury began to hit the panic button on the cash register, worried that they weren't going to recoup on the band. Accusations of undue extravagance were directed at the Dolls, which Thau heatedly contested. "They were still in the red but that could change in a minute with just one record. The first record only cost $17,000 to make and the second wasn't much more than that." Each Doll still received $200 a week but it was hardly a queen's ransom. They got by in much the same way as they had before they signed to Mercury, pulling off little scams to bring in extra bucks, like charging Steve Leber for fake doctor's and dentist's bills. Jerry Nolan: "We didn't get no big steady money. We tried to take advantage of the situation the best we could. Of course we had limousines and ate in the best restaurants but we never had cash in our pockets."

The Dolls were an updated version of the Bowery Boys a.k.a. the Dead End Kids, a celluloid fabrication based on the adventures of genuine Bowery urchins. From 1935–58, dozens of B-movie Bowery Boy comedies were enjoyed by the American public. In his memoir of New York low life, Luc Sante describes the Bowery Boys as . . . "A troop of amiably rowdy adolescents whose good hearts were sorely tested by the temptation of the boulevard". The Dolls succumbed to temptation then went back for more, waving the occasional expense account in the wind. Eliot Kidd: "We'd all be sitting at a table in Max's, and The Rolling Stones or Led Zeppelin or The Faces or Mott would be

134

sitting at the other tables. It was an incredible time and no matter who was there, the most popular people in the room were the Dolls, which I think hurt them. People in Iowa had never heard of the Dolls but it was easy to believe from hanging out in Max's that they were the biggest band in the world. They thought they were as big as Zeppelin or Bowie and they weren't, yet those people were making millions of dollars. The Dolls were making $200 a week but they were spending more than that."

The New York Dolls were also terribly incident prone, and someone had to pick up the tab for all the broken mirrors, damage incurred while touring, invoices for stolen switchblades and black leather jackets. Bail had to be raised and hospitals paid. Thau attempted to reign in his charges from a dead end destiny. Marty: "I told them I saw drunkenness and stonedness and sycophants feeding their egos. I told them to start cleaning up their acts and to start writing new songs, otherwise they were going to be in serious trouble."

9

Lady Chatterbox's Lover

In May '74, The New York Dolls began a punishing three month trek across the US to promote *Too Much Too Soon*. It was the kind of schedule that would have broken the spirit of a crack platoon, never mind the boys in the Dolls. Peter Jordan: "We had to go far and we had to go fast, which was a complaint of many bands in that era. We used to fly everything, every passenger was allowed six pieces of luggage so we used to travel with 12 people and fly our equipment for free. Things diminished as time went on, we went from being bloated to small, then we kind of got smaller. Then we wound up going back to trucks."

Unlike Led Zeppelin or the Stones, the Dolls were unable to afford the luxury of a private jet to transport them in style but they came up with some amusing diversions to take the tedium out of travelling. Sylvain: "In those days Alice Cooper was fucking huge in America. Now if you had long, black curly hair like me and you spent time in airports, everybody would think you were Alice Cooper. They'd come up to you ... 'Are you Alice Cooper?' and I'd say 'Yeah.' 'Can I have your autograph?' 'Sure.' This one time we were on a jumbo jet and on board the plane there was a high school band. One of them came up to me and said, 'Are you Alice Cooper?' 'Yeah,' And I gave him an autograph. I was sitting next to Johansen, and by this point I'd signed five or six more autographs, so I said to the next kid that came along ... 'Oh by the way, this is Mick Jagger, don't you want his autograph, too?' During the five hour trip, every kid on the plane came up to get Mick and Alice's autographs."

With hardly a day or night off, the Dolls sped through Detroit, Lansing, Columbus, Cleveland, North Carolina, Ohio, Florida, Charlotte NC, Washington DC, Connecticut, Baltimore, St Petersburg and Michigan. Clearly, it had not been noted by whoever planned the band's touring agenda that without a break the Dolls tended to implode after any given two month period spent cooped up together. Arthur was the first to go running from the trenches into no-man's land, when the band arrived in Cleveland, Ohio. Sylvain: "Our career is going up and down and it's hard for us. There was an incident in Cleveland that further fuelled certain peoples' opinions of the band. We were in a hotel room, being visited as usual by every groupie in town, male and female, when these two girls start with their opinions . . . 'Last night, we were with Deep Purple and Arthur you are a fucking drag, man. Last night those guys destroyed a whole room for us.' So you know what Arthur does? He raises the window and proceeds to throw out the TV, and most of the furniture in the room. The next day I see all the stuff that Arthur had thrown out of the window smashed up on the landing of another roof. The hotel management gave us a bill for $500, of course that came out of the Dolls' money. Now our managers are using Arthur's rampage as an excuse to tell us that we are screwing up. When the management see David, he's really firm with them. They don't see him as the screaming bloody mess that we did."

In the plush uptown office of Leber and Krebs, there was an implicit if silent belief that even if the Dolls went down, Johansen wouldn't. Of all the Dolls, David was the most able to present a professional facade, backed up by an enormous personality and a slug of Remy Martin. David Johansen: "It's funny because as demented and high as I was, I was still responsible. I would be like, this guy or that guy is fucking up, what am I going to do?" He was like the driver of a runaway carriage, holding fast on the reigns as the horses leapt into the ravine. When the Dolls finally smashed into a million pieces, it was Johnny Thunders and Jerry Nolan who got the rap for ultimately taking the band over the edge but Johansen was drunk at the wheel. Cyrinda Foxe: "Sometimes he'd go on stage and he'd be so drunk he couldn't perform. He'd sit down and talk to the audience and they'd start throwing rolls of toilet paper and he'd start screaming about being thrown to the lions."

One month before his 22nd birthday, Johnny Thunders started to sauté his mind in uncut methamphetamine (also referred to as methedrine) and was never quite the same again. On June 15, the Dolls arrived in Canada, where some obliging Hell's Angels supplied Frenchy and Johnny with some pure speed. Peter Jordan: "No matter what Johnny got into, he got into it 100%. He was into baseball 100% as a kid. He was into playing guitar 100%. When he got ahold of methedrine, which is the strongest type of speed known to man, he got into it 100%."

Jerry Nolan and his old pal saxophonist Buddy Bowser, who accompanied the Dolls on their '74 tour, spent the afternoon scouring the pharmacies of Toronto for a bottle of Robitussin A/C, a codeine based cough linctus. Unable to find a bottle of Nolan's favourite legal remedy, Buddy and Jerry returned to the hotel. Buddy Bowser: "Jerry was pissed off, he had a headache. We were downstairs in the hotel lobby when he sees a magazine stand, with a little pharmacy connected to it. He was ecstatic, they had a whole counter full of it." Nolan and Bowser went upstairs to get ready for the gig and looked in on Johnny, only to find him gripped by amphetamine psychosis and refusing to go on stage unless Sabel flew out to Toronto. Buddy: "I went into the room to try and get him ready to go on stage, he's not dressed and the room is in a total uproar and he's going over and over, 'I can't find it, where did I put it?' Forty minutes later he found the methamphetamine stuffed in a toilet roll, where he'd hidden it. He had a whole bag of it, and he laid out a minute line and I was sailing like John Coltrane and ready to hit that stage. Just as I was about to sail out of there, Johnny goes: 'I wanna know if you can see 'em', and he leans three quarters of the way out the window and is pointing up at the next roof top, at a pair of sneakers that some guy must have thrown up there when he was drunk or something. Johnny thought they belonged to the FBI, who were up on the roof and had tracked him down. Me and Jerry cracked up. Johnny was going . . . 'No fucking way am I going out with those sneakers up there.' " The enterprising Mr Bowser called Sabel up in New York, and advised her to talk Thunders down. Sabel: "He was crying and calling my name. Then their road manager called me and said: 'Get here, somebody's got to watch over him.' " The gig went ahead as scheduled but Thunders' methamphetamine madness had not yet run its course.

Sabel arrived in Montreal to find her once fine Romeo clawing at the walls and anyone who came near him. He was sure that the FBI were still on his case, could envisage a stay on Riker's Island, chained up between the murderers and rapists. Miss Starr could do little to diffuse his fears. Sabel: "He was on the worst speed trip, I had to take some to stay up with him. He was high for days. He called down to the hotel desk about the FBI and I was sure the police were going to arrive any minute, he was so out of control. The next day we went out for lunch and this black guy walks past us and Johnny goes: 'Put up your dukes, don't be looking at my girlfriend.' I swear to God, I was so scared that the guy was going to take up the challenge and it was going to be like watching a dog get run over, if he'd got hold of Johnny. We went to this Italian restaurant and they had wine bottles on the wall and he says to the waiter: 'How much are the saddle bags?' Oh God, I just had to get him back to the hotel. The next day they had a gig in Syracuse and he didn't want to get in the limousine. I couldn't get him to do anything, he was so unruly. I'm surprised we ever got to the airport. Then boom, he crashed, he couldn't walk, he was in a coma. We had to get him on the plane in a wheelchair. Then he woke up and beat the shit out of me. It was the worst trip of my life."

It might have been a good idea to have the paramedics on stand-by as the walking wounded tour continued across Tennessee, New Jersey, Boston and Baton Rouge in Louisiana. A trip to England, scheduled for the first week in July, where the Dolls had been advertised as playing at Olympia in London and the Buxton Festival were cancelled, as was a one-off Scottish gig. It was a trying time for all UK Dolly devotees, especially Steven Morrissey who wrote to Laura Kauffmann at Mercury Records after the Dolls pulled out of their English commitments. Miss Kauffmann replied to Morrissey on July 30, 1974: "Dear Steve: I'm glad to hear that you'd found out in time the Dolls weren't going to London. They were very disappointed, but there had just been too little time for us to get everything together for the trip. Hopefully, it won't be too long before they really will be going over there. Of course that depends largely on how the record does over there, so I'm counting on you to get everyone excited about it. You must have all the fans write to papers and buy records and write to radio stations."

The Dolls got to New Orleans on July 17, only to discover the smouldering remains of the venue they had been booked to play. The New Orleans' Warehouse club had burned down to the ground and the band were left with a couple of free days in which to amuse themselves, until July 19 when they were due to appear in Fayetteville. Still high on methedrine, Thunders got into the jazz spirit of New Orleans. Peter Jordan: "He'd been up for days and he went out on the street and bought a trumpet and stand-up bass. He wound up getting high with the guy who'd sold him the instruments and then he had to return everything."

From Fayetteville, the Dolls travelled to Los Angeles, where they had a four night stand from July 23–26, scheduled at the Roxy Theater. Owned by the hugely influential music business impresario, Lou Adler, the Roxy was also hosting perform-ances of The Rocky Horror Show. Written by Richard O'Brien and eventually made into a feature film, The Rocky Horror

Show is a musical cornucopia of transvestism and warped heterosexuality that became a big hit with those who wouldn't dare attend a genuine transvestite revue but instead got their rocks off in the safety of actors playing a role rather than living it. The corseted and crimped members of the cast took immediate umbrage to the Dolls' road crew when they began setting up the band's equipment. Peter Jordan: "We get there and the place is full of actors and they had tape markers all over the stage and all this crap all over the place which had to be moved. The next day we find out that the actors had been complaining. 'They tore up all our tape off the floor!' 'Fuck You' was the first thing we said. We fell foul of the theatrical community and got banned from the Roxy. We were supposed to play four nights, we got booted out after only one. We were told that not only would we never play the Roxy again but we would be lucky if we ever got to play in LA again."

The cancellation of their run at the Roxy, which had sold out in advance, made the band the target of some disparaging local press comments. One publication subtitled a piece of misinformed tittle-tattle with 'The Roxy Theatre Told The Gotham Grotesques To Pack Up And Go' and claimed that the Dolls had arrived so late at the theatre that the proprietors had no choice but to turn them away and revoke the rest of their booking. It was all too easy to damn the Dolls without taking the evidence into account. They'd made their own bed and it was getting kind of hot and sticky. At a dinner party for the band hosted by the LA branch of Mercury Records, the Dolls showed up three hours behind schedule. In lieu of an excuse, Johansen proclaimed that 'Los Angeles stinks' before sitting down to dinner.

The only positive note to be struck during their aborted stay in California was a live appearance on the *Don Kirshner Rock Show*. The nationally syndicated concert programme was filmed before an audience in the Long Beach auditorium, south of LA, and broadcast on television across the US on a Friday evening. Kirshner, another big deal showbiz wheel, who would have looked more at ease presenting Burt Bacharach than the Dolls, introduced them on his show as 'One of the most controversial groups on the scene today' before leaving the crowd to judge for themselves. Despite all that had befallen them, the Dolls were on top form for the duration of their half hour performance which featured material off both their first and second albums, including 'Showdown', 'Stranded In The Jungle', 'Trash', 'Chatterbox', 'Don't Start Me Talking' and 'Personality Crisis'.

The Dolls' spot on the *Don Kirshner Show* was a victory in vain. When they returned to New York at the end of July, after a further two gigs in Ohio and Cleveland, they were well and truly in the soup, like drowning flies at a rich man's dinner table. While Marty Thau was still the Dolls' doting daddy, Steve Leber was refining his role as their strict uncle. Marty: "The invisible storyline to keep the Dolls down by the music industry had reared its head again. I was really angry that their gigs had been cancelled out in LA but what could I do? When I got back I went to Steve Leber's office and the first thing that greeted me was the comment . . . 'Well, the Dolls are dead in LA, now.' I said: 'As a matter of fact one of LA's biggest promoters saw them at the Roxy on the first night and thought they were great and he's prepared to book them in LA.' Steve Leber said that was bullshit and phoned him. We get the promoter on the line and he tells Steve how much he loved the Dolls and he was ready to book them at The Palladium which was a big venue. Leber's jaw dropped but that conversation was the beginning of some of the arguments between Leber and myself."

As the Dolls' star was burning up in the prevailing atmosphere, Aerosmith's tawdry sun was on the rise. Although David Krebs was the third partner in the Dolls' managerial trinity, he kept a low profile, spending most of his time on Aerosmith. Marty Thau: "Krebs was very quietly handling their management roster. Later on it seemed to me that he was watching the whole Dolls thing and when he or Aerosmith saw something that they could take from the Dolls, in terms of style, show-manship and musical riffs, they would. I've had my suspicions that Leber and Krebs wanted to keep the Dolls down 'cos Aerosmith were moving up and CBS was backing them."

Marty Thau vehemently disagreed with Steve Leber's decision to put the Dolls back on the club circuit. It was a punitive move that would further erode the band's ebbing morale. Not only had the Dolls divided into separate factions but their managers were now seriously at odds. Thau: "Leber said to me that the Dolls were failing and would have to go back to playing clubs. I had always insisted that we would never do a show where the band didn't headline or open for a major act. I approached it that way because the band were so good and that was the way to establish them. Then he tells me that he has a show for them in Michigan, now in Detroit they could pull in 5,800 people and he wanted to put them on in a club that held 900. I said: 'You can't do that, it's wrong.' Then he said: 'We're in a hole over a certain amount of money.' I replied: 'You make them play smaller clubs, you'll be putting the nails in their coffin.' "

It wasn't a case of lights out for the Dolls just yet but it was getting kind of dark around them. Especially for Johnny Thunders. Sabel: "It was horrible to watch a person go totally insane. He was getting crazier every day and the beatings were getting out of control." Somehow Frenchy and Johnny had managed to smuggle the methamphetamine back to New York and Thunders went into the grand finale of his speed frenzy. Sylvain was sitting pretty in the Greenwich Village basement apartment that he shared with his girlfriend, Janet Planet, when Thunders' sister, Mariann phoned. Sylvain: "She was very worried, crying, wanting to know what was wrong with Johnny. What had happened was somebody had come over to fix her house in Queens and Johnny had locked the maintenance man in the basement and run away, so I said that I would look out for him. An hour or so passed and who comes to my door but Johnny and he's got EYES. I mean they are bugged out of his fucking brain and he's so shaky. He is also extremely paranoid and talking this crazy talk . . . 'D'you see that taxi? D'you see who's in that taxi? David Johansen, he works for the CIA and the FBI, that was him right there.' I'm trying to calm him down, I get him something to drink, and I don't mean water, when he goes outside where my bicycle is and starts cutting the break wires, all the time talking . . . 'You see who just walked past there, that was David.' Everything was David, David was a CIA person, he's working for Nixon, all this crazy shit. I managed to get some valiums and gave him four or five 'cos he was so bugged out. Apparently he'd done a whole ounce of methamphetamine. Anybody else they would have probably been committed. After that, something burned out in him. He was never quite the same, it's like he got instant schizophrenia."

Shortly afterwards, Sabel Starr attempted suicide by slashing her wrists and was taken to Bellevue hospital by Sylvain. Given the choice by a doctor of either going into the psychiatric wing or going to live with her mother, Sabel returned to LA leaving a devastated Thunders to begin a long distance campaign to win her back.

Quite often, exhausted speed users will turn to heroin for the drug's tranquil embrace. Johnny Thunders was no exception and where before he had dabbled, smack became his primary drug of choice. It didn't help that the Dolls now had a dealer for a road manager, who would also deliver right to their apartments. Sylvain: "I hated that guy 'cos he made it so much easier, he practically served heroin to us."

The keen young guitarist who had rehearsed alone, long into the night, of his own accord, and had been briefly courted by Jimmy Page, who thought Thunders was on the verge of international renown, chose self-destruction. If he couldn't be the world's greatest guitarist, then he would be the greatest junkie. 100%. Eliot Kidd: "There was a point when Led Zeppelin were staying in New York and Jimmy Page would be offering to send a limo round to pick Johnny up. We had three or four weeks of great parties because Jimmy Page had a big thing for Johnny, he thought that Johnny was going to be the next special guitar player. If Johnny could have disciplined himself, he could have been that. It was just a matter of making a left when he should have made a right. He cried about it a few times. He put his image as a guitar player above his playing. Unfortunately then his image became self destructive and that's when it really fell apart."

On two consecutive Mondays in mid-August, the Dolls returned to Club 82, out of drag. New York's neon heart still skipped a beat whenever the Dolls were on show and the small venue was packed to the rafters, hours before the Lipstick Killers were due to take the stage. Even Max's had forsaken the band, when David Jo became the third Doll to be banished from the premises after tearing apart the back room and going for a flock of Eagles roadies who had made disparaging remarks about Cyrinda. "We haven't been so prolific lately," commented the Dolls' frontman when he sashayed into the 82. Chris Charlesworth, reporting for the *Melody Maker*, took the Dolls' pulse and found all was not was well . . . 'For the past two Mondays, the Dolls have appeared at the Club 82 in New York, an ideal place for premiering new 'glittery' talent in New York, but hardly the kind of venue for a band with two British tours and two albums under their belt. An obvious step down, in fact, and a sure pointer that all is not well in the Dolls' camp. Some observers are going as far as saying the Dolls' demise is a carbon copy of the Velvet Underground's story in New York. Perhaps in five years time, their albums will be hailed as works of art and David Johansen, Johnny Thunders and Co will be resurrected in much the same way as Lou Reed has made his recent comeback . . .'

Down at the 82, the Dolls got into full swing round midnight. Despite a growing catalogue of problems, they could always be relied on to throw a great rock'n'roll party. Arthur took over the lead vocal's for a rendition of Rick Nelson's 'Poor Little Fool' and an extended knockabout blues jam was augmented by Buddy Bowser and a member of Television, a rising young underground band. Chris Charlesworth signed off for *Melody Maker*: 'In a club, a small, sweaty, noisy, crowded basement like the 82, the Dolls are perfect. On a concert stage, exposed before the eyes of a few thousand, their imperfections stand out like sore thumbs. Perhaps that's why I finally understood the Dolls on Monday.' Their second 82 show on August 19 was curtailed by the arrival of police officers who slapped writs on the club management for overcrowding, and the disappointed Dolls were swept out like debris, into the night.

Arthur's vocal turn on 'Poor Little Fool', just like his earlier hidden plea in 'Private World', was a rare comment from the man once described by David Johansen as 'The only living statue in rock'n'roll'. Although Kane verged on being an inanimate work of rock art, this was one statue with limitations, and he was cracking. Elda Gentile: "Arthur was totally vulnerable and after the Connie incident, he was picking up on any groupie that could get close to him. The relationship with Connie had been devastating and he was drinking more and more." Not only did he lack steady companionship outside of the band but he no longer had a close connection with any one Doll. Arthur: "The group pretty much divided in half. We had David and Syl on one side who were ready to sell out and do anything to stay in the business, and then we had the rebellious side of the family, Johnny and Jerry, the teenage hoodlums . . . 'We don't care. We'll take junk and kick you in the face.' I'd been there since the whole thing started and it hurt me to be in the middle of these two factions that were going in opposite directions. David and Syl had each other and Johnny and Jerry had each other and I didn't have anything, really. I was just trying to keep it together but I buckled under."

When the Dolls began the final lap of their US tour, Kane wasn't on board. Instead, he stayed in New York in an attempt to recuperate. Once again, Peter Jordan deputised. "Arthur we left behind, he was in a rehab place. Arthur was never fired, or had his wages docked. He always got his salary and if he was left behind he was looked after."

Steve Leber carried out his plan of putting the Dolls on at smaller venues and their Autumn itinerary was sporadic and low-key, with minimal advertising or financial backing. On August 17, the band played the Joint In The Woods, in New Jersey, before travelling to the far flung reaches of Dakota, where they had gigs in Minot and Fargo. They got to Detroit on August 26 but the outside of the Michigan Palace no longer bore their name; instead Leber had booked them into the Trading Post for three nights. Peter Jordan: "We realised that things were going to shit but we thought that things could have been salvaged. We were still working and viable. The Dolls were not an arena band but they were one of the best bar bands you could ever see anywhere. I don't care if it was a redneck bar full of bikers or pansies in Paris, they could go into a place and win the crowd over, but it took a lot of money to keep the organisation on the road. You have to pay salaries and work often enough to justify that, and ideally sell records. A lot of money was poured into Alice Cooper and Kiss before they ever made a dime. Leber and Krebs didn't want to back the Dolls, they'd started making money on Aerosmith and Mercury was a dog, they were doing zip in terms of promotion."

To ease the Dollies on their way to oblivion, their friendly road manager was always on hand. Introduced into the Dolls' road crew at the suggestion of Steve Leber and given the okay by the rest of the management team, he served a year with the Dolls. Sylvain: "He was a nice guy and everything but he was instrumental for doing one thing, the dirtiest thing that could have happened. When we were on the road, he used to come to our rooms and sell us heroin. That might not seem like so much but can you imagine that Johnny is already sick the way he is. Usually he would have to behave himself because he would have to pick up in different towns on the itinerary and it wasn't all that easy. I mean this guy would call Johnny in his room, Johnny never got his per-diems 'cos he would always owe this guy money. Once I overheard him and Marty chatting. Marty said: 'How's Johnny going to be on the road?' and the road manager said: 'Don't worry, I'll take care of Johnny, there's not going to be no problem.' Of course he was taking care of Johnny. Johnny got so bad it became disgusting and Jerry got so messy. Jerry used to brag to me . . . 'Oh man, when you're on heroin, you never get sick.' "

Even when the band weren't on tour, their road manager made himself indispensable. Sure, it's easy enough to score in Manhattan but with someone willing to provide deals on wheels, straight to your door, there is no incentive to ever clean up. Sylvain: "I don't know if he was paid so low that he had to do something extra or if there was an agreement to take care of whoever wanted it. Even David got started on it, he used to do this thing called skin popping, you shove the needle in your ass, into the muscle and that's not a very pretty sight to see, either. So when Johansen says it was Johnny, it wasn't just Johnny. I have to admit that I did it too but I didn't use a needle, I started snorting it and that's how I know that this guy used to go to people's houses and sell it 'cos he came to my house, too."

Following a gig at the Minneapolis State Fair, on September 1, the Dolls returned to Manhattan. What they needed most was the stability of a united management but instead they got caught in a crossfire exchange of allegations and recriminations between Steve Leber and Marty Thau. "Leber was putting them in all the wrong places," says Thau. "They became so demoralised and their career was beginning to crawl. I was very sad to see it happen. I had told them what had to be done, Mercury said that they would put out another record. I said 'Let's get to work and stop playing rock'n'roll party, start playing rock'n'roll career.' *Too Much Too Soon* had reached 167 in the Billboard charts and sold 100,000 copies, a little less than the Dolls' début album. Although Mercury had consistently given the band the cold shoulder and done increasingly little for their career, they were still willing to allow them to make a third album, providing the Dolls demoed some new material.

Unfortunately, The New York Dolls were no longer a cohesive unit and there was no quick fix solution for a band who never compromised and could no longer compromise with each other. Once Mercury agreed to a third album, a flurry of meetings began. Sylvain: "Basically there was a big void. Our gigs started getting funkier and we weren't making much money and the management was feuding amongst themselves. Then they start to have meetings with us individually and as a band. At one of the last meetings, Johnny brought up David's drinking. Of course, David didn't think he had a problem and his ego was devastating. He wasn't going to change but Johnny gave him that chance and said to David: 'I'll change if you will.' We all knew everybody had problems. I've seen a lot of people on drugs, including myself, who have made comebacks but if you don't want to change as a person, you can't do anything."

Although the Dolls continued to rehearse when they weren't on the road, any songwriting was done individually. Johnny Thunders came up with 'Pirate Love' while Sylvain, who hoped desperately for a reprieve for the band and pinned his hopes on a new album, put forward 'Teenage News', a hold over from *Too Much Too Soon*, and 'The Kids Are Back', an anthemic slice of Dolly history. Even though Syl's compositions were frothier and flirtier than the old Johansen/Thunders numbers that were the mainstay of the band's repertoire, they were still representative of the Dolls. Peter Jordan: "I would wind up rehearsing all this material with Johnny, some of which would turn up with The Heartbreakers, like 'Pirate Love', but a lot of it disappeared. By then everyone had their own agendas, their own lives. David and Johnny became so fucking alienated they wouldn't work with each other but the real pain in the ass was David wouldn't work with Jerry if you gave him a million dollars. The other thing was Johnny had songs he wanted to do and David said to me one time: 'What am I supposed to do while he does his songs, play tambourine? I'm not going to do that.' "

Steve Leber began pitching ideas at the band, promising them a trip to Japan, if they cleaned up their acts and ditched Marty Thau. It was like asking a bunch of dysfunctional kids to choose between Ma and Pa. They couldn't. The warm torpor of heroin and the security of sucking on a bottle of booze insulated them from the reality of the situation and made them too hazy to act. Cyrinda Foxe: "I remember Steve Leber coming round, pounding at the door and David begging me to tell him that he wasn't at home. David was terribly immature and he'd turned into a drunk, what a crashing bore. He had no incentive anymore. When it turned bad with Johnny, he blamed Jerry 'cos Jerry was a lot stronger than Johnny. He was the one that would instigate and have more control over the situation and Johnny would follow."

Jerry Nolan had no wish to see the Dolls go down fighting. He'd been pleased as punch when he first got the gig and had been tight with Johansen but ... "David had a bad habit of calling the shots about things he knew nothing about." Nolan had been sorely tested by their front man's choice of producers and as a result the balance in personal loyalties had shifted. Within the Dolls there was now a total deadlock, and with their trigger-happy emotional reflexes exacerbated by copious amounts of drink and drugs, a cease-fire seemed highly unlikely. Jerry Nolan told *The Village Voice*: "Me and Johnny liked this idea of going to Japan and making a third album. Me and Johnny said, 'Look David, this offer ain't so bad. If we keep our fist together, we'll win. If we open our fingers, we'll lose.' That was it. Bam! David took offence."

All the lovely rented limousines had been driven away, leaving them to ride the subway train once again and like the lyrics of the song, they couldn't understand why their lives had been cursed, poisoned and condemned. Their glittering entourage diminished, as had the interest of the press and any forthcoming gigs were now advertised by lowly little flyers instead of the beautiful glossy promo posters that had once announced their live appearances. On September 13, they played two shows at Jimmy's on 52nd Street. There were no more extra thrills for their audience, just a free buffet to snack on before the Dolls came out and did their thing. They played Ebbet's Field in Denver then returned to Toronto on September 21. When they got back to Manhattan, Steve Leber called another meeting to remind the boys about the third album. Only David and Sylvain showed up. "Steve Leber started talking about these producers from Long Island who wrote lots of bubblegum songs, called Kastenetz Katz. Me and David went out to their studio and they played us this recording, it was bubblegum, la la la stuff. The song finishes and they go: 'Okay, this is going to be your next record. You guys don't have to do anything but be on the cover and I guarantee you million dollar sales.' Obviously we flipped out because it was so stupid and got the hell out of there."

Marty Thau, who couldn't bare to see his starlets stumbling down to skid row, made a last ditch attempt to get them back on course. After inviting Steve Leber, David Krebs and all of the band to a small bar, Thau watched the last of his Doll dreams get stubbed out. Marty: "There was confusion all around and bad blood was emerging between Leber and myself. I felt that I really had to call things to a head. The thing that bothered me most was putting them back on the club circuit. I told them: 'You are selling your souls for $200 and this thing is going to go down the toilet,' and I told Steve: 'You can't sell them out. Your perceptions on this are wrong. You should try to remember how you behaved when we started out, when you were doing the business and the bookings and follow that route once again. Your reading of their progress or failure is wrong. We've got to retune our merger and have some clarity.' He said that I was a Pollyanna – meaning that I was two-faced and I told him that he was too straight and moral, then he accused me of taking money from him to buy them drugs, which was outrageous. Leber created such a stink. Either the ship was going to sink or swim but I wasn't going to be the reason why it was going to sink. I said: 'Okay, you think you know what to do. I'm not going to sit here and fight with you. My life goes on and I have overheads to pay. Let's see what you can do.' " With that Marty and his wife left the little bar and the Dolls behind.

Marty Thau represented the humane face of management for The New York Dolls. Primarily he was still a businessman but he also cared for the band on a personal level. Sylvain: "No matter how bad Marty can be, he was the only guy that held my hand when I was crying over it all."

Meanwhile, Malcolm McLaren was back in town on business. Naturally he looked up the Dolls. Sylvain: "We hung out with him for a couple of nights and he couldn't believe that the Dolls were in such trouble and on the verge of breaking up." Still misty eyed over the band – and mortified by their predicament – Malcolm decided to extend his stay in Manhattan.

10
Trailer Trash

As 1974 faded so did The New York Dolls' hopes of making a third album. After the Kastenetz Katz caper, Sylvain, ever the cheerleader, tried to rally the band around by proposing that they make a demo of 'Teenage News'. A good deal sunnier in its outlook than the Dolls' usual frustration heartaches, it bounces along instead of grazing both knees on the sidewalk, tripped up by Thunders' erratic chaffing riffs, and the band had already rehearsed and performed Syl's chirpy composition. Jack Douglas, who had been the studio engineer on the Dolls' début album and who was now gaining prominence as a producer in his own right, agreed to work with the band on their demo.

Studio time was booked for the Dolls at the Record Plant but aside from David and Sylvain, the rest of the band were in no fit state to apply themselves to anything other than maintaining their individual habits. Jerry Nolan, hitherto a stickler for professionalism, showed up but got junk sick and left to score. Johnny never even made it to the session. Arthur arrived shaking in his boots from the DTs and was unable to play. And no 'Teenage News' was very bad news for the Dolls, at least as far as Mercury Records were concerned.

Disheartened by the failure of the Record Plant demo, Sylvain quit trying to get everyone to kiss and make up. Syl: "For me that was it. There was nothing wrong with the Dolls that couldn't be fixed but everybody stood their own ground. Johansen blamed Johnny and Johnny was like, 'Fuck you, you've got a huge ego,' and Jerry was behind the lines but yelling Johnny on, 'Yeah, you tell him.' "

On October 5, the Dolls played the Liberty Bell in New Jersey, then for the last time in their career made their way to Los Angeles, where they had a gig at the Hollywood Palladium, on Friday October 11. Advertised as the Hollywood Street Revival & Dance, the Palladium show also featured Iggy Pop, Flo & Eddie and assorted rock'n'roll riffraff, including Michael Des Barres, the singer from Silverhead who was now Miss Pamela's fiancé. The remnants of The GTOs promised to do a turn, as did local scenesters Rodney Bingenheimer and Kim Fowley. Even Sabel Starr came out of hiding. The bruises had healed and so had her heart. Sabel: "Johnny and I had stayed in touch for three months and I was still madly in love with him."

The scars showed through the sequins at the Hollywood Street Revival. Although the night was designed to conjure up a little decadent romance, it was one stop short of glitter to gutter. Richard Cromelin, writing for *NME*, felt the shiver beneath the chiffon: ' "If anything, it turned out to be a wake – though the attendance was better than expected and the show went off without any disasters (beyond various musicians missing in action in the cramped backstage corridor). It was a chance to claim survival, or to be frivolous under the spotlight one more time, or to cling tenaciously, with noble foolishness, to a sinking ship. It was a summit meeting of progenitors, legends, pretenders and successors." Cromelin reacted to the event like a reporter at a reform school reunion, taking notes and regaling his readers with titbits on matters such as Miss Pamela's forthcoming marriage and a role in a soap opera to rumours that Iggy was going to be working with former Doors keyboards ace Ray Manzarek. But as far as the Dolls' future was concerned, Cromelin picked through the ashes and predicted the worst: "The New York Dolls had played LA three times previously, and each gig had been disappointing, but just aggressive enough to make you think and hope that they'd have it together the next time. But there's no point wasting any more time. It's really a trash band, with a bad, mushy sound, and now a definitely tiresome image that can't hold them up much longer. More than any of the other acts at the Trash Dance, the Dolls are hooked to a time that's inexorably rolling away, and their only redeeming feature is the perversely fascinating way they suicidally cling to their path to oblivion."

When the Dolls returned to New York, Sabel went with them. Once again Miss Starr and Mr Thunders were an item.

It was winter in Manhattan and the Dolls were left out in the cold. The band had failed to deliver any demo material and Irwin Steinberg, the head honcho at Mercury, was demanding repayment on losses and loans they had incurred. Paul Nelson: "There was a pretty constant war going on back and forth between the Dolls and Mercury and I was aware of it because I was stuck in the middle. Money was at the core of the situation. I felt more for the band than I ever did for the record company, who had no real understanding. The turmoil always seemed to be about money and I didn't want to get involved in it, because I wasn't allowed to make any decisions anyway, so I don't know the actual figures or details but I bore the brunt of the turmoil because I'd brought them to Mercury. Mercury had never had a group like this before and they were very much a company that didn't want any waves being made on any level." There was no longer anything that Paul Nelson could do for the Dolls. As their crisis worsened, Nelson left his position at Mercury and returned to journalism, taking a job at the *Village Voice*.

Although Mercury didn't officially drop the Dolls until the following year, they withdraw any support towards the end of 1974. Donna L. Halper, the East Coast A&R director at Mercury, responding to a letter from Steven Morrissey inquiring about the welfare of his Dolly darlings, issued the following statement: "Since I know you like them, I am sure you won't agree with our reasoning but the reality is neither of their two LPs sold very well. Not only that, but they were costing us huge amounts of money because of their tendency to destroy property in hotels. I truly believe that the company tried to be fair and patient with the Dolls but as talented as they were they were a continued source of aggravation for us."

When Mercury pulled out Leber & Krebs also cut the purse strings but not their contractual ties to the Dolls, putting the band in an untenable position. David Johansen: "We were sick of those guys and I'm sure they were the same way about us. It's funny because I still have an affection for those guys but at the time, it was us against them. See, Marty Thau had been having trouble with his marriage and he went into Leber and Krebs for money and he couldn't pay it back so they took over the band. As a person in the band it made you feel like, 'I tied my horse to your wagon and now you're going to unhitch us and essentially sell us,' which is not too humanistic."

The Dolls drummed up some Christmas money by playing a couple of low-key dates, including Mr D's in New Jersey on November 2. A gig in Cleveland followed on the cusp of the festive season. There were no New Year's resolutions to be made, contemplating survival was enough to contend with. Peter Jordan: "Mercury faded from the scene in late '74, early '75. They wouldn't do any more for them. At that point Leber & Krebs said, 'Screw this. We won't put any more money into it either. We're no longer going to pay for any rehearsal time or equipment, plus you owe us money.' Because of the Dolls' original contract, Leber & Krebs ended up owning the band's publishing rights. Not only that, they owned the band's name. They owned everything you can own, they even owned the royalty rights."

For Johnny Thunders, who passed public comment only rarely since he felt events spoke for themselves, Leber and Krebs' treatment of the Dolls was just the first in a line of betrayals. Johnny: "I started the Dolls with managers who didn't give a fuck about us or our interests. They were just out for money. They showed me how cold and nasty people can be, and I just couldn't see what that had to do with rock'n'roll."

* * *

The Dolls' sole means of salvation now lay in the unlikely cradle of the London-based fashion designer who'd become their biggest fan. Witnessing The New York Dolls in their death throes, Malcolm McLaren was keen to offer mouth-to-mouth resuscitation and get them back on their feet. However, aside from all their personal, financial and contractual problems, the beleaguered Dolls were also now in a cultural void. McLaren: "Although there was still potential, they were a bit washed up. Washed up in the sense that they'd had their moment but their moment didn't happen. They'd fucked up. Their management didn't want to know, nobody wanted to know, there was so much fall out. The record industry didn't know what direction rock music was heading in. They were still trying to sell all these huge groups that had made fortunes in the Sixties. I suppose the Dolls fell under the low rent garage rock label with Iggy Pop and MC5, who weren't taken seriously. They weren't money-spinning groups, they were aggravation groups but the Dolls had an ability to strike a light and they had a following."

The Dolls were stuck between a rock and a hard place. They were looked on as street royalty by those involved in the burgeoning New York punk scene centred around CBGBs on the Bowery but as influential as the Dolls were, they didn't have a role to play – apart from being guest stars – in the new and austere artistic uprising. Photographer Roberta Bayley, who knew Malcolm McLaren from working in his shop while staying in London, became the door person at CBGBs and understood the Dolls' dilemma: "They were superstars of the downtown scene but they were not a part of the new thing. They were very innovative and they inspired a lot of those groups. For many of them, the goal was to be as big as the Dolls. It seemed like they were really big and in that small scene they really were famous and adulated. Musically they were more firmly based in R&B and rock'n'roll than the punks were but in New York, punk wasn't just one thing, there was room for Blondie and Talking Heads."

At the beginning of Blondie's career, Johnny Thunders and Eliot Kidd would often join them on the small stage at CBGBs, warming up the crowd during their first couple of numbers. Sabel Starr had become close friends with Debbie Harry and got to know others from the punk scene. Sabel: "Johnny and I had a honeymoon period, where he was very sweet to me. During that time we were seeing a lot of Deborah Harry and The Ramones started to come round as well. Debbie was great, she'd dye my hair, and I'd dye hers. Then the beatings started again, as the Dolls were really falling apart."

This time, Sabel left Johnny for good. "I was still in love with him but he was getting crazier. He was totally unpredictable. I woke up one day and thought, 'I like myself, I'm tired of being beat up. This is no way to live.' I was so young and naïve . . . it's a tough way to grow up, I'll tell you that much." Although Sabel's relationship with Johnny had gone to grief, Miss Starr had become idealised by some as the ultimate contemporary rock'n'roll girlfriend. One young girl just in from Philadelphia called Nancy Spungen attempted to emulate Sabel's style by similarly bleaching her hair and wearing it in loose curls.

Through January 1975, while Malcolm worked on a resurrection package for the Dolls, the band continued to play the odd gig. The Coventry in Queens and My Father's Place in New Jersey just about kept them ticking over financially, as did the discovery that they could claim unemployment money. The fastest boys on the block were reduced to standing in line waiting for welfare. McLaren put down what little cash he had on a loft on 23rd Street where the band could work up a fresh set and store their equipment. The Dolls shared their newfound rehearsal space with Eliot Kidd's band The Demons, while Frenchy used the loft as his living quarters.

Although Malcolm McLaren has often been referred to as the Dolls' manager during their final days, it would be nearer the truth to suggest that he was their willing helpmate. Sylvain: "We never had any paper with Malcolm, no signatures, nothing, but he's always claimed that he was our manager.

Basically, he was our friend and he started to take care of a little of our business." The Dolls had very few options left. No one from the cigar sucking music business establishment would have touched them, or even come within fifty yards, but McLaren was optimistic and he cared. He could also furnish them with a new wardrobe. David Johansen: "I know he says he was our manager but he wasn't really. He was our haberdasher."

As far as Sylvain was concerned, this was a chance to get the Dolls up and running again. He could feel the energy coming off the punk scene and wanted The New York Dolls to get with it. Although they came from a different perspective to the CBGBs bands, they were the same age. Syl: "All these bands were starting to take shape, like Television, The Ramones and Patti Smith. There was a change going on but we were still doing the same old fucking thing. We'd toured with material off the second album, some of which dated back to 1971 ... we were in 1975 now. I'd say to Johnny, 'Let's wake up, let's go!' He'd say through sleepy eyes, 'Oh man, fucking David.' 'Forget David. Clean yourself up. C'mon we were never like this.' It just got worse, all his love affairs got screwed up, Sabel had gone, he was messing about, running from one to the other. As for Arthur, I mean I love Arthur and I hate to be saying anything about him but his life really sucked. He would drink and drink and drink. Then drink some more."

Out of all the Dolls' waning commitments, a request from a Canadian television company to film the band sitting on top of garbage cans performing 'Trash' was the most poignant: Top Cat and the kittens wearing McLaren's red vinyl designs, singing for their supper. The 3D mini-movie they made, like so much of the Dolls' legacy, vanished into an archive vortex and no one can locate it. Bob Gruen: "It was one of the last things they did together as a band in New York, and Arthur was just crumpled in a corner in this five-dollar trench coat, like a homeless bum would wear. He looked like a bum, there was puke on his coat and he was curled up in a foetal position and

Johnny was saying to him, 'Arthur, you're passed out like a bum.' One thing about Malcolm, he really liked the Dolls, he really wanted to work with them but the last time he'd seen them they'd been the toast of London and Paris, everything had been fabulous and now they were wasted and wrecked. He didn't really manage them, he oversaw their demise so he could get them to wear his clothes a couple of times. What he did do, very much to his credit, was save their lives and gave them all a chance to go on and live."

After sorting out Arthur's medical insurance, McLaren escorted a trembling Killer Kane to Smithers, a top of the line alcohol rehabilitation clinic. During the bass player's stay, Malcolm visited every day and encouraged the rest of the band to do likewise. McLaren: "It was astonishing. I was being so naïve. I didn't know what I could do. Yes, I could dress them up and help them but how do I address Arthur and his problems? How do I address Johnny and his drug problem? How do I address David who wasn't the star he was supposed to be and pissed off because of it. Who was he pissed off at? The rest of the band, of course. I thought, 'What am I going to do with this crowd?' So I walked into their rehearsal room, like a professor coming in with a cane and said, 'Right I think we need a complete reassessment of the entire band. You've got to change everything. Not just your habits but the songs and we've got to change the way you look. Let's face it you're a bit out of date.' "

Like Professor Higgins in *My Fair Lady*, McLaren set about rehabilitating the Dolls. But while Johnny Thunders had the doe eyes he was no demure Audrey Hepburn and Jerry Nolan was from another movie altogether – *The Blackboard Jungle*, in which the professor gets jumped. Jerry Nolan: "Malcolm's just a parasite. He observed the Dolls and what they were up to, and he was smart enough to know what they had, what sold, what kind of potential we had and he used up everything he learned off us to put his own group together." McLaren had his heart in the right place, but he also had his mind in gear and Nolan could sense it. Needless to say, Jerry and Johnny resisted any attempts by McLaren to intervene in their personal habits, though they did see a doctor.

In spite of all the calamities, the Dolls rehearsed hard and worked up sufficient material to go back on the road with a brand new set. Most of the songs, like 'Funky But Chic', 'Girls', 'It's On Fire' and 'Red Patent Leather' were Johansen/Sylvain collaborations but David and Johnny did manage to deliver one low-life ditty entitled 'Down Town'. In desperation there was democracy, and solo efforts such as Johnny's 'Pirate Love' and Syl's 'Teenage News' and 'The Kids Are Back' were included in the play list. Otis Blackwell's 'Daddy Rollin' Stone' was also adopted as the Dolls' latest cover choice. If Mercury Records hadn't been so hasty in retracting their offer of a third album, the band, with the right care and attention, might have survived.

David and Sylvain had already written 'Red Patent Leather' by the time Malcolm decided to dress the Dolls like the rent boy division of the Chinese Red Guard. McLaren's inspiration didn't come from out of the blue, it came out of the red. Johansen: "Because 'Red Patent Leather' was a good song, we thought we'd use it as our schtick, y'know 'Red, you're the judge/Red, you're the jury'. We had that and we thought, 'Hey, let's dress in red leather'. That wasn't Malcolm's idea, that was our idea."

Malcolm McLaren then sent some designs, along with the Dolls' measurements, back to Vivienne Westwood in London. Although the band's new wardrobe was all made in the same scorching shade of red, each outfit was unique, right down to their red shoes. Rather than just using leather, Westwood incorporated vinyl and rubber in the collection, taking inspiration from both the gay and S&M scenes. Zips were sewn into skintight vinyl tops and accessories like chain necklaces with their own amyl nitrate bottle holders completed the look. Perhaps if Malcolm had stopped right there, and not politicised the red theme, the Dolls might have got away with it, but when it came to burning bridges, the band were experts. Peter Jordan: "Have you ever seen *I'm Alright Jack* with Peter Sellers? Malcolm was like some sort of labour hold-over. It was a Labour party, power to the people type thing with him but you couldn't meet a more capitalist motherfucker in your life. Nonetheless, he loved the idea of Communism. He liked the posters and the graphic realism of the socialist movement. He liked the surface of Communism but God forbid you should try to get a buck out of him."

The next stage of the plan was to get the Dolls gigging again. They would relaunch themselves in New York before heading out on the comeback trail. Malcolm took the situation into his own hands when he secured the band four dates between February 28 and March 2 at the Little Hippodrome. Situated on East 56th Street, the theatre had a capacity of 2,000 and was more familiar with drag shows and stand-up comedy than rock groups, although The New York Dolls combined all three elements. The Little Hippodrome was out of the Dolls' usual venue circuit but that suited McLaren just fine, even if it proved a little disconcerting for their old fans. Malcolm: "I'd met some guy who looked like a young hippie from Harvard, nothing to do with the downtown drug scene. He was a completely nice, middle-class American kid who thought it would be really groovy to do something creative in rock'n'roll and had a nice big club uptown. I didn't want the Dolls playing in CBGBs, it didn't look very commercial and I didn't fancy speaking to the people that ran it. They looked a bit rough."

In the meantime, Sylvain set about organising the rest of the Dolls' campaign. He bought McLaren a map of the States and contacted his cousin Roger. Sylvain: "There was a cousin of mine who used to be in The Vagrants, his name was Roger Mansoeur and he booked us a tour of Florida, going all the way from Tampa to Miami. Up and down the coast. Florida is its own animal, it's a huge place. First we open up at the Little Hippodrome, then we go down to Florida, get really good with the new songs, play all the clubs and get really hot 'cos once we get back to New York, we can't fuck up anymore."

Hearing of the renewed activity in the Dolls' camp, Leber and Krebs once again became interested in the band and summoned McLaren to their office, ostensibly to discuss contractual details but also to issue a timely reminder that the Dolls' former managers still retained complete ownership. Undeterred, Malcolm got busy finalising the rebirth of The New York Dolls, and issued a press release: WHAT ARE THE POLITICS OF BOREDOM? BETTER RED THAN DEAD. Below was written: "Contrary to the vicious lies from the offices of Leber, Krebs and Thau, our former 'paper tiger' management, The New York Dolls have not disbanded, and after having completed the first Red 3-D Rock'N'Roll movie entitled *Trash* have, in fact, assumed the role of the 'People's Information Collective' in direct association with the Red Guard. This incarnation entitled 'Red Patent Leather' will commence on Friday, February 28 at 10 PM continuing on Saturday at 9 and 11 PM followed by a Sunday matinee at 5 PM for our high school friends at the Little Hippodrome. This show is in co-ordination with the Dolls' very special 'entente cordiale' with the Peoples Republic of China. New York Dolls, produced by Sex originals of London, c/o Malcolm McLaren."

Malcolm took the Communist Party image further by insisting that all tables in the Little Hippodrome should be draped in red fabric and even suggested that every drink sold while the Dolls were appearing should have an injection of red dye. The major theatrical gesture, aside from the band, was a huge red flag bearing the hammer and sickle which would be hung as a backdrop behind group. There was no real empathy between McLaren and Johansen until the flag concept. Sylvain: "Johansen and McLaren never got along until they clicked on the making of the flag. They both had political leanings." Cyrinda Foxe got out her sewing kit. "I sewed that flag, I made it in the apartment on East 17th Street. I wanted to do it because it was so weird looking and I had nothing to do, but boy was it a nightmare. I thought the outfits were great but a little too glitzy and I didn't think the Communist flag was a good thing to have behind them, they could have done some kind of Chinese symbol instead, but they always took the most destructive path. They were making a statement that this country was not quite ready for."

In much the same way that the cover of the Dolls' début album had been judged at face value, without humour or perception, so was their Red Party, and once again the band lined up to face the moral firing squad. As Paul Nelson later noted in an article in the *Village Voice*: "Somehow all too many people again failed to recognise the Dolls' nihilistic, riffraff sense of humour . . ."

Acting as support at the Little Hippodrome were Pure Hell, an all-black punk band and the innovative Television. At the request of the Dolls, Wayne County agreed to be the guest DJ. Wayne: "Their real decline was with Malcolm McLaren. He made them like horrible cartoon characters, dressed in their red leather outfits. When they débuted the Communist look, I was deejaying. Every time I'd play a song like 'Psychotic Reaction' (by Count Five) or 'Liar Liar' (by The Castaways) the whole audience would go 'Yayy!' I'd put on The Seeds and it was 'Yayy!' knocking them out, then David walks over to me with a Communist Worker's album and asks me to play some of it before they go on stage. I didn't know they were going to do anything like that and I didn't want to play it, people were going to think it was me but I had to put it on. 'Power to the workers, power to the people. The workers will not bow to the capitalists . . .' The whole audience went 'Urghhh' and I was sitting there giving the audience looks like they are making me do this. Then the curtains opened. Everyone wanted to love them 'cos it was the Dolls but there was no cheering. Everyone thought it was stupid, not real."

Once again, Peter Jordan deputised for Arthur who had relapsed. Wearing an outfit that had been cut for Kane, Jordan sweated in rubber trousers three sizes too big for him. Arthur only played the last date out of the Little Hippodrome run and Jerry Nolan hit the floor after the second show. While Nolan was tucked up in rehab, Spider, Pure Hell's drummer, did the honours. David Johansen clutched a copy of the Maoist handbook like a Bible and wondered who was going to be the next in line to fall. In the face of adversity – in reality the only face they'd ever known – the Dolls performed as pluckily as ever. Unfortunately, the band didn't sound totally at ease with the new numbers and neither did the audience who lit up only when the Dolls broke into established favourites. Even their choice of covers – 'Daddy Rolling Stone' with its call and response treatment and Eddie Cochran's 'Something Else' – were somehow not fully integrated. Sylvain handled Clarence 'Frogman' Henry's anthem of the stateless, 'Ain't Got No Home', with great gusto and Johnny's treatise on the needs of the opposite sex, 'Pirate Love', was a bundle of raw energy but the shows failed to take the audience anywhere near the climactic level of old. Like their new clothes, the Dolls hadn't quite grown into the material. Paul Nelson: "It was a disaster. Everyone kept waiting for them to play something that they knew. The songs weren't so good and they only played one old Dolls' song. I only saw one of the shows. It was very strange, you didn't know if it was supposed to be funny or not. They only played about six or seven songs so it was a very short show."

The two teenage girls who had fervently supported the Dolls since the Mercer Arts Center and had worked hard establishing a fan club for the band in NY, run independently of Mercury Records, walked out of the Little Hippodrome with their heads bowed. If McLaren had staged the Dolls' red uprising in Europe, the audience's sensibilities might not have been so ruffled, but 56,555 American soldiers had died in Vietnam attempting to stem a Communist take-over. It was too much of a sore point for most to understand the intended irony of the Dolls' attire. Lisa Robinson, a journalist who had fiercely championed the band, gave them some pointed advice. Sylvain: "She said that in America, you can be gay, you can be a drug addict but of all the taboos you cannot be a Communist. Malcolm's mistake was to put up the flag. We could have still had the clothes and the songs but if he'd really had management talent, he would have seen what was going to happen. It kamikazed our whole thing. We'd crossed the line one too many times."

The Dolls had only just survived being labelled gay transvestites and had the bruises to prove it. If they were going to pursue the Communist trip under Malcolm's regime, Vivienne was going to have to run up matching bulletproof vests. Bob Gruen: "Malcolm liked the way the Dolls had stirred things up with their gay prancing but the way to really attack America is to pretend that you're Communists, then see what happens. Trying to stir up Communist anger was dangerous because the people who didn't like Communists pretty much didn't like anybody else and they could get violent about it. In England, when somebody gets violent, they punch you in the head. It's a lot more dangerous here, you can get shot."

The New York Dolls thus became Malcolm McLaren's prototype for testing public reaction. Later he would claim they were faulty goods, too fucked up to be workable, but they would have been decimated had they continued with the Communist theme in the States. McLaren had failed to correctly gauge American attitudes. When he launched his next group, The Sex Pistols, under the banner of anarchism, he was on reasonably safe turf with the cold-blooded English. There hadn't just been a terrible war fought in the name of anarchy.

Backstage on the opening night at the Little Hippodrome, the fake fur on the Dolls' scarlet boas started flying. Malcolm McLaren: "Lisa Robinson got terribly upset. I overheard her talking to Lenny Kaye, who was in Patti Smith's band. She was saying, 'It's disgusting what's going on with this group. Their manager is a Communist, he's going to change everything.' Meanwhile some guy said to Johnny Thunders, 'Well are you a

Communist then?' and Johnny said, 'Yeah, do you want to make anything of it?' What showed me the difference between Johnny and David was that Johansen ran and hid in the toilets before rushing up to Lisa Robinson going, 'You don't understand, it was just a load of fun.' He poured water on the wine until you couldn't taste the wine anymore. What he said was unforgivable where I come from but I'm not American. I suddenly saw the differences between the American and English people. In England people see Communism as an ideology, in America it freaks them out."

In early march, the Dolls hoisted their red sails into the sunset and made for Florida. Due to a lack of funds, Peter Jordan had been fired and remained in New York, but after only 24 hours on the road Kane once again became incapacitated and Jordan was flown out to cover for him. Following a week-long booking in Tampa, wearing the same red vinyl & rubber outfits night after night, they headed for Hollywood, next to West Palm Beach for a gig in a club called The Flying Machine. With an entrance constructed from a B52 bomber, the date provided a little light relief thanks to a party of budding Sharon Stones. Sylvain: "It was a big club, a sit-down place with seats at the front, and a dancing area behind. The front row was taken up with all these young girls in mini-skirts and as we started to play, they all lifted up their skirts. We were looking at them and they weren't wearing anything underneath. Frenchy of course started blowing on his whistle ... 'Okay you and you and you, c'mon backstage.' Those girls knew how to have a party. It was always fun with us tho', never abusive."

In keeping with the new political image, the Dolls took to wearing army surplus fatigues during the day. A boy can get heatstroke dressed in tight fitting vinyl in the swampy Florida climate. To McLaren, the tour was an awfully big adventure. For the band, especially Johnny and Jerry, swatting mosquitoes and playing dives was no fun. However, there where moments *en route* to gigs when, unified against the

167

threats of the locals, Malcolm felt his little platoon were going to make it. McLaren: "We were travelling by car and it was still pretty redneck down there in the South. It was KKK land and we'd hit a town and get stopped by a group of guys who'd threaten to call the sheriff if we didn't get out of the car. Clearly you did not want to step out of the car, you just pushed your foot right down on the accelerator and sped out of town and on to the freeway as fast as you could, without stopping. These people were crazy. You didn't know what was going to happen. You could get the shit beaten out of you or end up in a swamp, ten feet under and it was at those times – and only those times – that you really did feel like you were part of a gang 'cos if one of us went down, we were all going down so you stuck together."

Base camp was Ma Nolan's trailer court in Crystal Springs, outside of Tampa. Peter Jordan: "When I say a trailer court, you would be hard-pressed to visualise this is in England but it was definitely from the wildest *film noir* fantasy. Jerry's mother and step-father were living in a frame house and they have a trailer park with about eight of these little trailers that look like grasshoppers without legs set around a court and that was it." Jordan, who was sharing with Arthur, was rescued by a hospitable local girl. "After being there a few days I couldn't take it anymore. I had met a girl. I wanted to stay in a house with air conditioning. I didn't want to sleep next to Arthur, he was a drying out alcoholic, in a trailer with no air conditioning and then have to eat dinner in Jerry Nolan's mother's house. I wanted to stay with this girl in her air conditioned house, smoke pot and then meet them at the club, when we had a show."

Unlike Jordan, the Dolls had no option but to tough it out in the broken-down trailers, listening to the midnight cries of sub-tropical wildlife in the neglected wilderness just outside their doors. Sylvain: "Jerry's mother had just got married to this really hick, abusive Yankee husband, y'know . . . 'Y'all in The New York Dolls, why y'all wearing make-up, y'all faggots?'

and he has a motel made out of trailers and this is where the Dolls are staying, being hung up on heroin and needing booze and not getting along, in 105 degree weather. It was horrible and we're playing these little shitty, dinky assed clubs. It's like in *The Blues Brothers* when they have to go and play in front of the good ole' boys, chicken wire on the stage, that's the kind of places we were fucking playing. Malcolm, he couldn't take it either but he's going . . . 'C'mon boys, come on, pleeaase', like a little British schoolmaster."

Thunders and Nolan had managed to stave off withdrawal, mainly through the efforts of a young fan called Jim Marshall who was scoring on their behalf. The deal went awry when Marshall's friend and connection was busted. As if the scenario wasn't already bad enough, Johnny and Jerry started to get junk sick. All of Ma Nolan's down home cooking that she provided for the band, from the big bowl of corn to the fried chicken and mashed potato with gravy, couldn't stop her boy's cramps and sniffles. David Johansen: "She was a real old sweet Irish woman, like Jimmy Cagney's mother in *Public Enemy*, 'There's no such thing as a bad boy.' "

The New York Dolls' infamous last supper was played out over Ma Nolan's dinner table. Sylvain: "We were sitting around eating, by the grace of Jerry's mother. We couldn't afford shit 'cos we're only making $100 a gig and Johnny and Jerry were really getting bad. Those poor guys, they were sick and getting sicker because they didn't have anything and I was getting kind of itchy myself, when Johansen goes crazy. In front of Jerry's mother, Johansen starts with . . . 'I'm sick and tired of this, everyone is replaceable, I'm sick and tired of trying.' He starts whipping them with his mouth and it was the last verbal whipping they were going to take." While Johansen continued to chomp on his chicken, Nolan pushed back his chair. Jerry: "I got up and said, 'I'm out.' Then Johnny got up and said, 'If Jerry's leaving, I am too.' " Nolan and Thunders promptly returned to the tin hell inferno of their trailer to work out their next move.

No matter how scrambled the rest of the band got, David Jo was always hard boiled. "They were Jonesing* but we had these gigs that we wanted to do. They weren't great gigs but it was a life and they were, 'We don't want to do these gigs, we want to go back to New York and rehearse.' I was like, 'Rehearse what? We play every fucking day.' It just got to a point – if you guys are going to split, then fuck it, y'know. It was the end of the run. If we had been a big hit and we were making lots of money, we could have probably kept it together but it was really just us at that point."

David already knew he wasn't going to be stranded. Being a Doll had become a permanent headache. Why bother when a brand new gig was just a phone call away. David Krebs had made it clear that if Johansen wanted to pursue a solo career, he would be taken care of, while Steve Paul, guitarist Rick Derringer's manager, was a good buddy.

For Arthur, who watched everything through glazed, sad eyes, Nolan and Thunders' sudden departure still came as a jolt. Kane: "I was shocked when Johnny and Jerry cut out but to tell the truth, if I had been more interested in heroin, I would've gone with them. Johnny and Jerry had this little club going with Richard Hell, the bass player from Television, who used to tell them how wonderful and influential heroin use was – 'You too can hang out in Edgar Allen Poe's apartment on heroin.' "

While Jerry's mom cleared away the dishes, her son called the airport to sort out a couple of flights back to New York. Jerry and Johnny packed up their belongings and threw them in the back of the band's rented station wagon. Sylvain put his foot on the gas, and Malcolm accompanied them to the airport. McLaren: "It was all a bit sad. It was only noble Sylvain who still wanted to pursue it and dearest Arthur, who was in hell."

It was late evening when they got to the airport. Pushing

* Old American slang for drug withdrawal.

their way through bustling tourists, Sylvain and Malcolm walked Johnny and Jerry up to the check-in desk. It was a subdued departure with little left to talk about. Sylvain: "Finally I said, 'What about The New York Dolls?' Jerry turned around and said, 'Fuck The New York Dolls' but he didn't mean it like, 'Fuck Off' . . . that's been misinterpreted, what he meant was, 'Look what's driven us away from the band. David's voice at the dinner table . . . "Hey man, I don't need you guys, I could go on on my own." ' What Jerry meant was all the things leading up to his and Johnny's leaving. Johnny, he didn't say a word. There is always a good and a bad to everything. At that particular moment, there was nothing good. What was good was left behind in people's memories. There was no sleeping on the situation and getting back together in three weeks because now Johansen had the chance to go out and get the band he had always wanted."

Aftermath
Broken Dolls

When Johnny Thunders and Jerry Nolan returned to New York, leaving the rest of the Dolls in Florida, they carried with them the vague hope of a reconciliation. It was never to be. The remaining Dolls played the last three dates on their Florida itinerary, hiring local guitarist Blackie Goozeman and a drummer to fulfil the bookings. Goozeman, who would eventually change his surname to Lawless and find heavy metal infamy with Wasp, would make much mileage out of his three-night stand with the broken Dolls. "Having known the members of the band, I waltzed right into the situation – 20 years old, babe in arms. Completely inexperienced, but it didn't take long. Baptism by fire. By the time I got in The New York Dolls, the band was on its last legs. They were struggling for existence. It was virtually over by the time I joined. I was only completing a formality," he told *Sounds* magazine in June 1983.

Once the gigs were done and dusted, the remnants of the Dolls scattered. Arthur Kane was given the band's amplifiers as a final pay off. Unable to face returning to New York, he threw in his lot with Goozeman and together they went on to form Killer Kane. Arthur: "I didn't want to go back to New York after the failure of the Dolls. It's funny how things change, you can be on top of the world and 30 seconds later, someone else is the next big thing and you get swept under. Disco music had got big as well, which was aggravating. I went to LA for about a year, and had a group called Killer Kane, then I went back to New York."

Peter Jordan cashed in his plane ticket and spent a further

two weeks in Florida before hitching home. Back in the city, he took a job doing sound for Wayne County. Following one of County's gigs at the Little Hippodrome, Jordan almost died from stab wounds while attempting to protect his wife in the course of a particularly brutal mugging.

David Johansen returned immediately to New York. He was uncertain about the future but he knew for sure that it wouldn't include Johnny Thunders or Jerry Nolan. Cyrinda Foxe: "All of a sudden David was back. He was drinking all the time and complaining that everyone was out to get him. The Dolls had been like a family to me, it had been really good but David no longer wanted to be in the Dolls. He would not make up with Johnny and Jerry. Syl wanted them to get back together, so did Steve Leber but David didn't want to."

Sylvain and Malcolm McLaren drove to New Orleans in the band's rented station wagon. McLaren: "It was wonderful. We saw all these old rock'n'roll guys singing in bars like Clarence 'Frogman' Henry and The Coasters. I had a great time but I caught venereal disease which was awful. These girls would just grab your arm and fuck your brains out in New Orleans. It was the first time I'd ever caught such a thing, I felt really awful and ashamed but I didn't mind, it was all part of the rock'n'roll trip and lifestyle and I was very happy to drive all the way back with Sylvain to New York."

During their impromptu vacation, McLaren reassured Sylvain that if the Dolls couldn't be mended, he had something waiting back in London. Sylvain: "As we were running around New Orleans he told me not to worry about stuff. He said he knew these kids that used to hang around his shop and that I could put a band together with them, teach them. Not to take off from the Dolls but to start something new. I was into it up to the point of giving him my Les Paul guitar and electric piano, then he was going to send me a ticket to London. I even wrote him out a phoney receipt so that customs wouldn't bust him."

When Johnny and Jerry arrived back in Manhattan, the bells

were tolling for the Dolls. The dissolution of the band affected few: only the devoted went into mourning. Even the band members themselves didn't quite know just what they'd lost. In a moving elegy to the group that appeared in the *Village Voice*, written by Paul Nelson only weeks after their demise, their stalwart supporter noted: "The Dolls broke up in the final weeks of April, the legendary desserts having forever eluded them. If truth be known, the news of their death hardly produced a ripple throughout the nation they sought to win. Their demise was taken as inevitable. The dreams of rock'n'roll's Dead End Kids burned out like a green light bulb on someone else's marquee and nobody particularly noticed any loss of illumination."

As if he needed one, Sylvain got an unsubtle reminder of the break-up when he dropped Malcolm off at his 20th Street apartment. Sylvain: "I remember this so fucking vividly. We had this really schmucky kid called Elwood, he was the last guy who wanted to work for the Dolls, Malcolm had found him and he used to drive us around. Elwood was the kid with the tattoo of the girl on his arm that said 'New York Dolls – Rock'n'Roll'. He rented a room right across the road from where Malcolm had been staying and as I was giving Malcolm his suitcase, Elwood looks out of his window and yells at us, "You guys broke up, you fuckin' assholes!""

The first band to rise from the ashes of the Dolls were The Heartbreakers. Assembled by Thunders and Nolan, The Heartbreakers were a mean and moody combo that looked at life from the downside; the open celebration of the Dolls now translated into vicarious kicks. An early publicity shot of the band taken by Roberta Bayley, which featured them with bloody wounds around their hearts, bore the legend 'Catch 'em While They're Still Alive'. Bayley's boyfriend, Richard Hell, joined The Heartbreakers on bass guitar after he quit Television. Ironically, Hell was also approached by David Johansen who was looking to set up a new incarnation of the Dolls. Roberta Bayley: "Richard had just left Television and was floating around when David asked him if he wanted to join the Dolls. We went to this club called Ashleys to meet up and have a drink with him but then Johnny and Jerry asked Richard too. Richard didn't want to be in another band where he was just a side person who didn't have a say in things, which ended up being the conflict in The Heartbreakers, anyway."

The New York Dolls were at the epicentre of McLaren's vision that would be projected on to the Sex Pistols. Another key source of inspiration that Malcolm would take back to London with him was the messed-up street kid look, as epitomised by Richard Hell, a style created from a wilful and poetic poverty. Even Hell's take on youthful nihilism, which he summarised in the song 'Blank Generation', inspired The Pistol's inferior 'Pretty Vacant'. Sylvain: "When we got back to New York, Malcolm fell in love with the punk movement. He studied it all. He got to know people by offering them things. He gave Richard Hell a beautiful blue Teddy boy two piece suit but to be honest, I don't think he ever wore it. Not because it wasn't nice but Richard was into his little ripped T-shirts, and Malcolm took that idea back to London with him. In London you could really do something with it, but here it doesn't get further than New York. Do you think kids in New Jersey would wear ripped T-shirts? It's a huge country. In America, at that time, the country was just getting out of Vietnam and the people were happy about their government, whereas England was entering a depression."

Between catching the clap and running out of cash, McLaren was itching to return home. By selling off sample designs out of the back of the station wagon and hitting Frenchy for two months rent money to sublet his old apartment, he raised the air fare to London. Once Frenchy discovered that he'd been duped by McLaren and the landlord had already secured new tenants, Eliot Kidd and a bunch of friends armed with baseball bats set off to teach the conniving little Englishman some NY street etiquette but McLaren had already fastened his seat belt. When he landed at Heathrow, he received an eager reception. Malcolm: "Steve Jones and Paul Cook were at Heathrow to meet me and here I was with Sylvain Sylvain's cream coloured Les Paul guitar with all these little cheesecake pin-ups on it. Like a mad man, I gave it to Steve Jones and said, 'Go and learn how to play it and if you can't play it maybe we can get some guys from New York to help you.'" Jones would make a profitable sideline flogging umpteen cream coloured guitars, swearing like a street market trader that the guitar he was selling was a unique, never to be repeated offer, as played in The New York Dolls.

The next project to emerge from the shadow of the Dolls was the new New York Dolls a.k.a. The Dollettes. This partial reformation was triggered initially by a Japanese pal of Bob Gruen's called Yuya, who had turned up in Manhattan eager to offer the band a couple of high paying dates in Japan. David and Sylvain visited Peter Jordan who was still recovering in hospital and offered him the gig. Jordan: "David and Syl came to see me and they said, 'We're going to Japan in August and you're going to come with us, we're going to start a band and call it The New York Dolls, again.' We had to keep the name to do the gig in Japan. When I got out of hospital, we hired Tony Machine. Tony had been fired by Leber & Krebs after his attempts at being our road manager were so inept but he was a good drummer and still works with David to this day. We also hired a keyboard player, Chris Robison, who had been in a band called Elephant's Memory."

Sylvain decided to go to Japan rather than London, despite McLaren's frequent exhortations. Syl had already talked to Johnny Rotten, Glen Matlock and Steve Jones on the phone and received a seven page letter from Malcolm, which is now on exhibit in the Rock and Roll Hall of Fame in Cleveland. Sylvain: "When Malcolm went back to London, he sold my electric piano, which is how they could afford to rent their rehearsal place in Denmark Street. He kept bugging me to come over and I was saying, 'Malcolm, I don't have any money whatsoever, why don't you send me a ticket?' 'Sylvain, you can sell another of your guitars.' All I had left was my White Falcon guitar. In the letter he'd included little photo booth pictures and he'd written things on the back of them ... 'This is Johnny Rotten, he could be the lead singer ...' 'This is the guitar player, Steve Jones ...' They were wearing hats and looking nice, not at all like Sex Pistols. If anything Johnny Rotten looked like Patti Smith with a haircut, in her early days. They looked like a nice bunch of schoolboys who'd steal your wallet. That was my impression of them and I thought I was going to have to teach them everything."

Utilising most of the Johansen/Sylvain numbers that had made up much of the set at the Little Hippodrome shows, the New Dolls played a 10-date Japanese tour which included an appearance at Tokyo's Korakuen Stadium, supporting Jeff Beck. David Johansen: "We made a lot of money. Well, it wasn't really a lot of money but it was for us, I had maybe twenty grand and instead of the manager being paid, they gave the money to us."

While the New Dolls were in Japan, the old Dolls' contract with Mercury quietly expired. Johansen and Co. returned to NY invigorated. David Jo took Paul Nelson to task for writing the *Village Voice* obituary and commented to the English press that, "The Dolls never did break up. We just got rid of ... uh ... a couple of people just left, that's all and I had to spend the next three months telling everyone it wasn't true. Which was very taxing." Despite gigging around Manhattan on a regular basis for a year, the New Dolls didn't get very far. Peter Jordan: "Chris Robison quit, then we hired Bobby Blaine and played with him until the band just drifted apart. No one would touch us with a ten-foot pole and The Heartbreakers got very popular. It was well known that Johnny and Jerry were total dope fiends and if two of the world's biggest dope fiends just left your band, then what does that make you? Plus David had pressure on him from his clique of friends who were suggesting that he go solo, which he did. Then Chris Robison and I started a band called Stumblebunny, we made an album for Phonogram and Syl and Tony Machine started The Criminals with Bobby Blaine."

The New Dolls appealed neither to the majority of the original band's fan base nor to a fresh audience, whereas The Heartbreakers became the leaders of the pack on the Max's/CBGBs circuit. Initially, Johnny Thunders had offered Eliot Kidd the post of second guitarist in The Heartbreakers but Kidd passed on the chance, leaving Walter Lure to defect from The Demons. Eliot Kidd: "When The Heartbreakers formed, Johnny had it in mind that I was going to be the fourth guy but I turned him down. Man, that was the stupidest thing I ever did in music, in my life. Walter was playing in my band but his style didn't really fit our music. We talked it over one night and he joined The Heartbreakers."

Managed by Leee Black Childers, The Heartbreakers continued to conquer their home turf, but Richard Hell was getting antsy. Johnny Thunders: "Richard had this thing . . . kinda an ego thing, I guess. He wanted to sing all the songs himself. It wound up with me gettin' one song a night to sing, and Walter gettin' one song a night, and Richard doin' all the rest. I'd had it with that number. I'd backed up a front man long enough."

The conflict within The Heartbreakers couldn't have been eased by Hell's budding relationship with Sabel Starr, who had begun to split her time between LA and NY. Sabel: "When I started dating Richard Hell, I would stay with Nancy (Spungen). She was a wannabeSabel, everybody hated her, she was so obnoxious but I didn't care, I had a place to stay. I tolerated her and even kind of liked her. She said she was going to London to get herself a Sex Pistol. Johnny and I had a love/hate thing. When Richard wasn't around, we'd get together and talk. I always used to tease him about sex and he'd say I had a one-track mind. I told him that would be a good name for a song. Everyone was doing heroin, we were all strung out."

In April '76, Richard Hell quit The Heartbreakers to

front his own band, The Voidoids. His replacement in The Heartbreakers was Boston born Billy Rath. Sabel Starr left New York for good and although she would maintain relationships with many of her rock'n'roll friends, she kept a quieter profile. Sabel: "I remember being totally disgusted with the scene. Punk rock was really coming in and I didn't care for it although I did like The Sex Pistols. When I left New York at 19, I vowed I would never go back and I haven't. I went home, back to the very exclusive place where I'd grown up, went back to school, got on the tennis team and got back to normal."

Unlike Miss Starr, Cyrinda Foxe turned her face up to the spotlight and bloomed, landing a significant role in *Bad*, one of the last movies to bear Andy Warhol's name on the credits. After tying the knot with David in 1977, Mrs Johansen slipped into the arms of Steven Tyler, whom she married the following year. Cyrinda: "I stuck behind David as much as I could but it was over so Steven Tyler got me, what can I say? Steven's always claimed that he stole me from David. He used to say, 'I saw you with David, I wanted you, I got you.' Oohh mucho macho!"

Cyrinda wasn't the only asset Tyler poached from Johansen. Aerosmith's frontman also pilfered elements of David's inimitable Dolly style. Cyrinda: "The Dolls were famous for their look, they had some really theatrical, fun costumes. They played dress up and Steven Tyler could see that. There is one Aerosmith album cover that shows Steven Tyler in a glitter outfit that is a complete knock-off of David Johansen." Dude looks like a Doll.

Arthur Kane was also hearing wedding bells. After the dissolution of Killer Kane he returned to New York and married his girlfriend, Babs. Following a spell in L.O.K, he got the Corpse Grinders together with Rick Rivets in 1977. Rick Rivets: "Arthur came up with the name, it was from a terrible Herschell Gordon Lewis movie. We couldn't find a singer until Arthur came up with this guy Stuie Wylder, who'd been in High School with us. Stuie lived right across from CBGBs, and was neighbours with The Ramones. We used to rehearse in his apartment and we could hear The Ramones playing through the wall. We did have a keyboard player but he wound up getting shot by the cops. He was selling guns out of his apartment and the cops raided him and they had a shoot-out."

The Corpse Grinders played the rounds of Max's and CBGBs for two years but failed to gain momentum outside of the underground scene. Coming on like zombified storm troopers in chalky make-up and black arm bands, which some construed to have a fascist symbolism, didn't help their cause, although they did record one album with Kane in the line-up for the small French label, Fan Club. Arthur was terminally crushed by the Dolls' demise and found it hard to trust anybody in the music business, even his old friends. Rivets: "I don't know why Arthur wasn't satisfied with the band. We did a lot of gigs, I think it was having to start from scratch again. We had to book our own motels and load our own gear, all that nonsense and he had a chip on his shoulder about the Dolls, he thinks everybody's out to rip him off but we were always straight with him."

If The Corpse Grinder's image was considered off-putting, it was The Heartbreaker's bad boy reputation that prevented them from getting a stateside deal. The Heartbreakers projected an awesomely powerful vision of life on the line and no record company wanted to do business with them for fear of getting burned. Public opinion pinned the breakdown of the Dolls on Thunders and Nolan and this, combined with their open love affair with heroin, ensured that Johnny would never again secure the backing of a major US record label. It was the intervention of Malcolm McLaren that saved The Heartbreakers from continually chasing their own tails in ever diminishing circles around Manhattan. Thunders and Co. knew little about The Sex Pistols but accepted McLaren's invitation to join their Anarchy Tour. The Heartbreakers flew out to London on the same day that the Pistols made their infamous appearance on Thames Television's *Today* show and engaged Bill Grundy in a round of verbal fisticuffs.

No self respecting UK punk was unaware of The New York Dolls' legendary legacy and many a black leather jacket was sprayed with their lipstick logo. In 1977 Mercury Records even put out a double album re-issue of *New York Dolls/Too Much Too Soon* in the hope of cashing in on the resurgence of interest. Johnny Rotten attempted to trounce the Dolls when he penned the irate rant 'New York' – "Pills/cheap thrills/Anadins/Aspros anything/You're condemned to eternal bullshit/You're sealed with a kiss'– but it was nothing more than an impotent tantrum over a mythology that pervaded the Pistols' camp.

When Thunders and Nolan arrived in London, they were given underground celebrity status by the bands and fans alike. The Heartbreakers made a huge impact on the English punks but would later stand accused, alongside Nancy Spungen, of introducing heroin to the scene. But it was hardly the fault of The Heartbreakers that Miss Spungen followed them across the Atlantic in ardent pursuit of Jerry Nolan. Rebuffed by The Heartbreakers, Nancy homed in on Sid Vicious, the Pistol who wanted to be a Doll.

Eventually, The Heartbreakers landed a deal with Track Records, drawing a conclusion to Kit Lambert and Chris Stamp's original interest in the Dolls that had been tragically aborted by Billy Murcia's sudden death. The Heartbreaker's début album *L.A.M.F. (Like A Mother Fucker)* was well received but the muddy production afflicted the already volatile nature of the band.

Out of all the various off-shoots from the Dolls, David Johansen's solo career garnered the most public acceptance. Aside from the odd flash of the old quirkiness, Johansen turned out a fairly conventional body of work. After signing with Steve Paul's Blue Sky label, with whom he would release five albums, David hit the road with Sylvain and The Staten Island Band. Sylvain continued his musical alliance with Johansen with the understanding that Steve Paul would later fund some Criminal's demos. The Criminal's had already cut one 45,

'The Kids Are Back'/'The Cops Are Coming' on their own Sing Sing label but the band were eventually iced when Sylvain was hurt in a car accident. When he recovered, he signed a solo deal with RCA in 1979.

The Heartbreakers went through a messy separation at the close of 1977, amidst infighting and Track's slide into bankruptcy, the Who having by now ditched their former managers *and* record label. Although The Heartbreakers split up they never finalised the divorce and would continue to regroup whenever the rent was due. In '78, Johnny Thunders signed a solo deal with Real Records who had also shown an early interest in The Criminals. With the release of Thunders' solo effort *So Alone* it appeared for one brief moment that commercial success in the UK was in reach. Unfortunately not enough copies of the single, 'You Can't Put Your Arms Around A Memory'/'Hurtin'' were pressed up and the album lost its momentum. Aside from the inclusion of two Dolls' tracks, 'Subway Train' and 'DownTown', *So Alone* contained 'London Boys', Johnny's retort to Rotten's 'New York'. Accompanied by Steve Jones and Paul Cook, Thunders' sneers: 'You telling me to shut my mouth/If I wasn't kissin'/You wouldn't be around/You talk about faggots/Little momma's boys/You still at home/You got your chaperone'.

It would certainly have been wiser for Sid Vicious to have stayed home but at the time *So Alone* was released he was in New York facing a murder rap over his beloved Nancy following the infamous Max's showcase where Vicious was backed by Jerry Nolan and Arthur Kane's outfit, The Idols. Nolan had attempted to keep a paternal eye on the couple and had even introduced them to his methadone programme but no one could pull them back from their awful final act. When Malcolm McLaren used the Dolls as the prototypes for The Sex Pistols, he forgot to erase their proclivity for misadventure.

In 1977, the US magazine *Punk* decided to run a special feature on The New York Dolls. To coincide with the issue,

Roberta Bayley wanted to reunite the Dolls for a photo shoot, on the exact spot in front of the Gem Spa, where they had posed for the back sleeve cover of their début album. After several failed attempts to get all the ex-band members together at the same time and place, Bayley succeeded. While she set up her camera, Johansen wandered over. Roberta Bayley: "I remember asking David if he and Johnny were still friends and he said, 'C'mon, we went through the war together.' "

Afterlife
The Mythic Link

These days Times Square is a tourist-friendly area. All the love parlours and peep shows have been boarded up and closed down by law enforcement officers at the behest of the city's moral guardians. Next came the property developers, more avaricious by far than any John that once cruised Times Square looking for a little cheap relief. It's a different kind of New York than the one in which the Dolls came of age. Max's Kansas City is now a delicatessen and although the Gem Spa on St Mark's Place is still standing, there is no plaque commemorating the band that made it a landmark for their fans. Behind the till in a nearby second-hand record shop there rests a small, ragged picture of the Dolls that someone has taped to the wall. A Billy Doll is now a mass-produced Barbie boy toy, 10 inches of blond muscle-bound plastic aimed at the gay consumer. Drag Queens are part of mainstream culture, Ru Paul has her own television show and Wigstock, a grand parade of fabulous Queens, takes place every Labour Day in New York, attracting media attention and tens of thousands of spectators.

The world keeps turning but The New York Dolls fell off long ago. Unlike The Velvet Underground, there have been no great posthumous accolades for the Dolls, possibly because they were too flamboyant and too flippant in their attitude for the so-called serious rock or cultural historians to concentrate on them for more than a paragraph or two. They have become rock'n'roll's great stepping stone in that their contributions cannot be ignored but they are all too often hastily skipped over in the scramble to get to The Sex Pistols. In his book *Fashion*

+ *Perversity*, Fred Vermorel barely acknowledges the Dolls in regard to McLaren and Westwood's creative development, commenting merely that, "He (McLaren) had some vague idea he would manage The New York Dolls and turn them into something special." Yet there are those for whom the memory of the Lipstick Killers is indelible. In 1984 Tony Parsons delivered a late lamentation to *New Musical Express*: They looked like they had crawled from the rubble at the end of the world. They were my first, my last, my everything. A lot of people – nearly everybody – thought they were laughable. Nobody came out and said it but the implication was there – the Dolls were heretics, perverters of the True rock and roll Faith. Why, they acted as though anybody could get up there and do it!"

Steven Morrissey grew up and with the advent of The Smiths got over the Dolls: "Five years ago I would have lain on the tracks for them, now I could never possibly listen to one of their records. It was just a teenage fascination and I was laughably young at the time. I always liked the Dolls because they seemed like the kind of group the industry couldn't wait to get rid of. And that pleased me tremendously, I mean, there wasn't anybody around then with any dangerous qualities, so I welcomed them completely. Sadly, their solo permutations crushed whatever image I had of them as individuals."

The likelihood of The New York Dolls' story having a happy ending was as slender as their grasp on the machinations of the music industry. In their afterlife, only David Johansen has attained any real commercial success, most of which came his way once he metamorphosed into a suave cabaret descendant of Cab Calloway known as Buster Poindexter in the mid-Eighties. David Johansen: "For six years I really worked, gigging every night. All of a sudden I was sitting in the back of the van, sucking on a bottle of gin at four o'clock in the morning, thinking 'This is not a life' and that's when I started the Buster thing. I'd been playing to crowds of kids pumping their fists in the air like a Hitler Youth rally, screaming for 'Funky But Chic' for six years so I used the name Buster

Poindexter and that way I figured people wouldn't be screaming for 'Funky But Chic' anymore." Johansen also eased his
way into films and television, carving a niche as a character
actor with a comedic flair. Since quitting drinking it would
seem that the only area of his life to which he has not become
fully reconciled is his role in The New York Dolls. He gives the
subject short shrift. "I had a great time and I loved those guys.
What more is there to say? It was kind of like a project and we
pretty much wrapped it up. I really had a ball."

Prior to his Poindexter metamorphosis, Johansen was playing at a large open-air festival in Belgium that included on its
bill both Chrissie Hynde and Simple Minds. To liven things
up, he got in touch with two old pals. Sylvain: "I'd gone on
tour with Johnny in 1984 and I was still seeing Johansen
occasionally, when he'd grab a new song or two off me. He
called me in Paris and said he would love for me and Johnny
to do the shows. He was doing two shows over two nights. Me
and Johnny travelled on this damn train to the gig and Johnny
was really sick. He could have died from any time onwards
from 1981, it's amazing that we had him up until 1991. Anyway
we got to the festival and that first night on stage Johansen
didn't even introduce me and Johnny, we just came forward at
the very end of the gig. I don't know what the hell happened
to that guy, he made such a 100 degree turn. He is a very
talented person and he's also been very lucky and very successful. I helped him get there, Johnny helped him get there.
Everybody that was in the Dolls helped him get there. Who
knows what would have happened if he hadn't had the Dolls
as his first vehicle, if you want to call it that. Although he's
done a lot of great things, the greatest thing he ever did was
The New York Dolls and it cannot be duplicated."

While promoting a new album in the early Nineties, David
Johansen was filmed by MTV tossing copies of the Dolls'
records into a river. The faded feather boa of Dolldom hangs
around his neck like a phantom mantle and he cannot shed it,
no matter how much he might wish to.

After Sylvain was dropped by RCA in 1984, he took on the full-time role of single parent to his three-year-old son, O'dell. Syl: "I drove a taxi cab in New York for three and a half years. When David Johansen played a taxi driver in *Scrooged*, I was getting mugged on the street."

David Jo was the only Doll given the opportunity to come in from the cold, but even if the door to acceptance through compromise had been held open for Johnny Thunders and Jerry Nolan, they would probably have kicked it shut. Marty Thau: "Johnny and Jerry were not able to pull off The Heartbreakers with the élan that the Dolls had. They were a good band but they ended up in the midst of nowhere bookings and ridiculous press stories. When they went into The Heartbreakers they were full of confidence that they were going to go on to something greater but they didn't have the informed understanding of what had to be done by others for them to make it happen. They became just another punk band playing clubs in London and New York. Later on they regretted it because in 1983 or '84, Jerry came to see me and started talking about getting some help in putting the Dolls back together but I knew that David didn't want to do it and with the evolution of Buster Poindexter, he didn't need the aggravation."

Johnny Thunders had no option but to continue playing the ultimate rock'n'roll outlaw. There was no place else left for him to go. A brilliant guitar stylist of the same calibre as Keith Richards or Wayne Kramer, Johnny's lowlife reputation cast a dark shadow over his attributes. After Billy Murcia, Thunders became the second victim of the Dolls. He never truly recovered and the descent of The Heartbreakers from a supreme rock'n'roll gang into a bunch of itchy fixers sealed his fate. Cyrinda Foxe-Tyler: "I loved Johnny. I always adored him and when I was having a low point in my life, he was there for me. Me and Johnny we were old friends and we used to hang out together back in the Eighties. I'd go to his shows and one time I said I'd meet him at the Mudd Club. I got there and asked someone where Johnny was ... 'Oh, he's in the bathroom, shooting up.' He was supposed to be on stage in 45 minutes. It was hot, dirty and I didn't like any of the people there. Finally he came out of the bathroom and he was fried, he played a horrible set. I noticed the way his following had turned into a 'Johnny Thunders' crowd' and he was catering to them. I was angry with him for letting them get away with it. Sometimes he would cry and tell me how he wanted his life back, then he would turn around and do drugs. We were out somewhere, and this girl ran up to him and tried to put some pills in his mouth, that was the in thing to do. Shove drugs down his throat."

Beneath the street aesthetics, Johnny Thunders had a heart full of soul which he deadened by self-medication. He toured continuously, not because he wanted to but, in the absence of a major league record deal, he had no choice. It became a pathetic rite of passage for any budding musician hoping to gain credibility by association to get high with Johnny Thunders. In 1986, he stated: "I would never advise anyone to start using heroin. All it does is fuck you up, y'know? But at the same time, I ain't no fucking preacher either. I ain't gonna lecture people on how they live their lives. See, I was very young when I started using heroin. Young an' innocent and I thought I knew it all, right? But I didn't know it all and I'd never have conformed to it even if I did. I had nobody to warn me off, to tell me it wasn't right. I guess I was about eighteen when I started using heroin. I tried it and liked it, and in some ways I don't regret ever having used it. I ... I loved taking drugs, right? I thought I was having a real good time, taking drugs and playing rock and roll ... but I wasn't. I only realised that when I started playing without drugs. See, for me, it's much the same at the end point anyway, I can play great without drugs, but I can play great with drugs, as well. It's real easy to start. It's when you come to stop you find out you got problems. Like, I've had to go on all sorts of methadone programmes and it's, well it's horrible. You find that you get to kinda depend on drugs in certain situations, and it's much harder having to deal with them straight; but really drugs just cocoon you."

Despite numerous attempts, Thunders never really managed to clean up; it was better to be numb than lucid. Sylvain: "His addiction was so overwhelming. One time he was playing a gig and he got sick backstage and a needle broke off in his arm but the promoter didn't give a shit. There was a crowd out there that had come to see Johnny Thunders kill himself on stage, anyway. The promoter dragged him out by his fucking hair and threw him on the stage. Johnny was up there for half an hour holding his arm. That was the gig, blood all over his sleeve."

All the dope stories have clouded Thunders' immense contribution to rock'n'roll and his influence often goes uncredited. Bob Gruen: "Johnny Thunders is now one of the most imitated guitar players around. People who don't even know who Johnny Thunders is are copying somebody who copied Johnny. There is no note that Steve Jones ever played that Johnny didn't play first. With all due respect, Steve Jones does it well, it's like Eric Clapton plays Robert Johnson. I once told Johnny I thought that he was the Chuck Berry of his generation. He was messed up one day and I was telling him he ought to clean up and that he was an inspiration for so many people. I took him to the Tattoo club on the East side of New York, they have rock'n'roll nights there, and Johnny asked me to introduce him to the owner, so I told him how great a guitarist Johnny was, the Chuck Berry of his generation and Johnny said, 'I also do an acoustic set, I'm kind of like Bob Dylan, too!' "

Even if Johnny T had never played a note, his rooster bouffant has so often been emulated across the years that this alone is worth a posthumous decoration. Sylvain: "I said to Johnny, 'If you had a nickel for every time somebody copied your haircut in the Dolls, you'd be rich.' "

The New York Dolls grew up in a high risk, live fast milieu and many of the protagonists continued their lives in a seam-less sweep to self destruction, a legacy that continued with the punk movement. Arthur Kane's ex-girlfriend Connie Gripp, who went on to have an equally explosive relationship with Dee Dee Ramone, died on the street while working as a prostitute in 1990. Cyrinda Foxe-Tyler: "She overdosed, it was horrible. I yelled at her once, when we found out she was screwing around on Arthur, with Steven Tyler. I remember she had a green chiffon scarf dress on and high heels and thinking how grand I was, I said something to her like, 'You have some nerve, you bitch.' She put me right in my place, she said . . . 'You have no idea what life is about.' She told me I was a beautiful girl and how could I possibly know. The way she said it was like a slap in the face. I almost apologised. She really taught me a lesson. It was a terrible awakening, I never thought anyone was different from anyone else, I never thought anybody wasn't on an equal footing."

Arthur Kane has lived a life in pieces, held together by faint hope. In 1989, he toppled from a window and smashed both knees. Sylvain tried to mend the situation by negotiating with a promoter who promised two gigs, one in California, the other in New York, for $25,000 per show to be billed as The New York Dolls, minus Johansen. Sylvain: "Arthur was all bandaged up, he was a mess. I thought it was a suicide attempt because he'd been so depressed but he was into doing the gigs. Then I called Jerry who was living in Sweden and he was definitely into the idea, and I spoke to Johnny. Everything was go. I'd been living in Toronto so I came back to New York. Then I saw Johnny outside the Pyramid Club and I said to him, 'Don't you remember why I'm here? We talked on the phone.' He was so out of it. He looked like he'd been wearing the same clothes for I don't know how many days, he looked like Ratso Rizzo in *Midnight Cowboy*, so bad . . . and he was carrying all his clothes in a black plastic bag, the kind you put the trash in. He couldn't remember anything of what I'd said to him about us playing together again, he didn't know what the hell I was talking about."

Out of the failed attempt to reunite the Dolls, Sylvain and Jerry Nolan banded together as The Ugly Americans. Johnny and Jerry hadn't played together for some time and Nolan was keen to get a new project underway. Jerry was a courageous character and an unsurpassable rock'n'roll drummer but his stamina was failing. Jerry: "There was a time when I used to be a good fighter in my heart and soul. I usually won my battles. This is the first time I ever lost a battle. I had a very hard time losing the drugs battle. It was hard for me to take but I found out a lot about myself, too."

After playing several packed out shows at the Continental Divide in New York, The Ugly Americans got a booking in Connecticut. Sylvain: "We were playing in a bar full of people who'd come to see us. We gave the audience a good show and if Jerry would have had the energy, we would've stuck together. He thought that we'd get a record deal in two or three weeks, but sweetheart, it never happens. He was really ill and we were on stage, that day he'd been unable to get anything. We're in the middle of playing and I saw Jerry's dealer indicating to Jerry from the front of the crowd that he hadn't been able to get him anything. Jerry didn't even finish the song. He tried the next number but couldn't keep the beat, then he just walked off in the middle of the set. I got mad, maybe said a few things but I figured, the poor guy, he just can't do it. His heart was in it but it was twenty years too late."

The New York Dolls might have pioneered the seductive image of boy sluts in glamorous rock'n'roll ruin but the reality is hazardous and it doesn't make for happy endings when you're forced to scratch out a living on the fringes of the rock business. Guns N'Roses attempted to adopt a similar pose but with the cushioning of a sympathetic and efficient record label, it wasn't too far for them to fall. Aside from David Johansen, who was pardoned, the other members of the Dolls spent the rest of their lives paying heavily for three years of glory.

After he was jumped from behind and attacked with a baseball bat while walking home during the LA riots, Arthur Kane got left for dead on the street. He was in hospital for almost a year and now has a metal plate in his head.

191

Johnny Thunders died alone and unattended in New Orleans, on April 23, 1991. He had been hoping to put a new band together with Jerry Nolan and Swedish guitarist Stevie Klasson but his failing system, combined with a cruelly conducive set of circumstances, finally caught up with him. The obvious conclusion was that he overdosed, and although methadone and cocaine were present and duly recorded by the coroner, the former New York Dolls' guitarist was suffering from a form of lymphatic leukaemia. Prior to leaving for a short tour of Japan a month before his death, Jerry Nolan tried to convince Johnny to go into hospital. Nolan: "It was the day before he was supposed to go to Japan. There were a couple of things that I didn't know what they meant, odd places for bruises to be, on his back and chest. I didn't find out until weeks later, that was the leukaemia. I started to talk him into forgetting the gig, I tried to tell him we had to go to the hospital. I told him I would have stayed. We would have got a private room, that I'd be in the room with him, or sitting outside the door. I almost got him to do it, then he got scared. He just got scared of needles, doctors, hospitals, the whole bit. You may not realise this but most junkies are afraid of needles. I told him he was going to die." The two friends last saw one another on 14th Street and 3rd Avenue, the same New York corner where Jerry met Johnny back in 1972 when he went to collect his Dolly trousseau, the day after he joined the band.

Life for Clyde was hard without Bonnie Thunders. Cyrinda Foxe-Tyler: "At Johnny's funeral, Jerry cried on my shoulder, 'What am I going to do? My best friend is dead. My soulmate has gone,' and I was like ... 'Jerry, you've got to survive for you.' " With the help of his girlfriend, Phyllis Stein, Jerry almost made it. He took great pleasure in restoring a 1972 Triumph motorbike and was delighted by the publication of his memoirs *My Life As A Doll* which appeared in the July 16, 1991, edition of the *Village Voice*. He hoped it would lead to a book deal. Jerry Nolan died in New York on January 14, 1992. After becoming seriously ill with pneumonia and meningitis,

Jerry suffered a stroke. Following Thunders' demise, Jerry asked Johnny's sister if he could be buried close to Johnny. His request was granted. They can be found in St. Mary's cemetery in Flushing, their grave stones strewn with press clippings and little tokens left by fans.

The Dolls are long dead, it's safe to embrace them. They were carried out on a stretcher back in 1975, their platform boots peeking out from beneath white sheets. They feathered their sleaze pit in candy pink satin and couldn't crawl out again, even when the party was over. The music business never forgave their effrontery. Marty Thau: "Now we're in 1997 and all the dust clouds have settled. Yes, I hate Steve Leber and he hates me but we did our best, we tried. Who were the Dolls? A bunch of drunks and drug addicts, they were wild kids but they didn't purposely set out to become drunks and drug addicts. They thought it was all in the flow and the game of the whole thing. Unfortunately, they were victims and that's why today, liberal as I am, as democratic and leftist, I'm equally conservative when it comes to drugs and alcohol, they'll do you in. The most important part of their story is that they were early pioneers of punk. The difference in what The Sex Pistols were doing and what the Dolls had done was not all that great. Because of the Dolls, the mainstream press were able to acclimatise to The Sex Pistols."

The New York Dolls were a self-destructive, hedonistic, split-second comet, a wonderful searing vision that liberated rock'n'roll. The Rolling Stones managed to escape from petty social constraints by attaining the kind of success that elevated them above every day rules and regulations. The Sex Pistols, barring Sid Vicious, were eventually financially remunerated and are now perceived as innovative instigators, with a slew of documentation attesting to their story. The New York Dolls just wasted away. Once Johnny Thunders died, his sister attempted to unravel the Dolls' contractual ties. Despite numerous album reissues, none of the band received any royalties since they split up until Johnny's sister began investigating. Mariann Bracken:

"I think the Dolls were taken advantage of. As far as they were concerned, they were making music, they were stars and none of them had a lawyer or any sense of what they were signing or doing. I'm doing this for Johnny and whatever happens will happen for all of them because they were a group and one effects the other so by me sorting it out, hopefully they will all get a share of what they were entitled to."

Sylvain: "I found out that The New York Dolls' publishing had been sold to Chappell Music, then they sold it on to Warners. There was an advance against the royalties but did anyone call us up to tell us?"

On a Johnny Thunder's tribute album, *I Only Wrote This Song For You*, released in 1994, a clean and sober Arthur Kane recorded his version of The New York Dolls' story, adapting a solo Thunder's composition, 'In Cold Blood': "They say our story will never fade/I just wanna know if we'll ever get paid/After our assassins are dead and gone/The New York Dolls will live on and on." Arthur: "After twenty or so years of waiting, I felt like everyone's died a thousand deaths. There is twenty year's worth of cassettes, vinyl, singles, anything you can imagine that hasn't been properly accounted for."

Marty Thau: "The Dolls were paid over $300,000 in royalties for the Guns N'Roses version of 'Human Being'. Warner Chappel only collect publishing earnings for Leber-Krebs, my publishing company and for the Dolls' publishing company, too. The Dolls get 75% of all publishing royalties earned and Leber-Krebs and I split the remaining 25%. Leber-Krebs and I lost lots of money in the Dolls' debacle . . . close to $150,000 which we'll never recoup but which we were legally entitled to from the GNR monies but chose not to in order for Arthur Kane, Jerry Nolan's mother, Johnny's kids and Sylvain to get something. The Dolls were tragic victims of the times, naïve, druggies/drunks, a great rock band, wild and crazy guys, foolish idiots, and mainly to blame for everything that exploded in their faces."

Sylvain Sylvain is still angry about the state of The New York

Dolls' back catalogue. When 'Personality Crisis' was used in a car advert, the moment was never capitalised on. A compilation album, *Rock'n'Roll*, was issued in 1994, but barely publicised. On the bootleg market, business is booming as usual and some of the best Dolls' products aren't strictly kosher. Sylvain: "The New York Dolls' career is alive but it could be doing a billion times better. It should be turned into a commodity but everyday we lose. There is nobody standing behind the cash register, there's nobody upfront to sell you anything and there's no one out back in the stockroom. Much as I hate the bootlegs, thank God for them because they've kept things going."

Despite the lack of a cohesive marketing strategy on their catalogue, references to the Dolls and the use of their material is kept alive, chiefly by memories and mythology. The 1994 movie, *Postcards From America*, a biographical account of the New York multi-media artist and gay activist David Wojinarowicz, utilises three Dolls' tracks, 'Looking For A Kiss', 'Trash' and 'Lonely Planet Boy', to great effect. The English film, *The Velvet Goldmine*, features a version of 'Personality Crisis', recorded by Teenage Fanclub.

A legion of bands and artists have been influenced by the Dolls in terms of style, attitude and in their approach to music. They include Aerosmith, Kiss, David Bowie, The Sex Pistols, The Clash, Japan, The Cramps, Hanoi Rocks, Guns N' Roses, The Smiths and D-Generation.

The New York Dolls are a part of modern culture, yet they remain obscure. They have become the mythic link, the mystery girls. Sylvain Sylvain: "Those six guys who were the Dolls, five at one time, five at another, there was nothing like those guys when they got together to do that simple thing – rock'n'roll. It changed all our lives. The greatest thing that can happen is that The New York Dolls keep turning people on, as we have done in the past. The only thing that kept me going when I had to drive a fucking cab and some schmuck in the back was giving me a hard time was that I remembered that I had something and people love me for it."

Cast List

Roberta Bayley. Most recently Roberta's pictures appeared in *Blank Generation – The Early Days of Punk Rock* (Simon & Schuster, US/Omnibus, UK). She still lives and works in New York and is recognised as one of the leading lights in capturing the NY punk scene on camera.

Leee Childers (a.k.a. Leee Black Childers). While toying with a death-wish fantasy, Leee told the author that . . . "Leee was walking down the street one night, when he saw a beautiful Spanish boy on a skateboard. As he skated in front of the bus, Leee dived to save him. The boy was saved and so was the skateboard but Leee was crushed under the wheels of the bus. In the words of the bus driver, 'He died a hero'. That was the end of Leee Childers. What's really happening to me is that I'm working in New York, as a photographer."

Jayne County (nee Wayne County). Wayne metamorphosed into Jayne at the close of the Seventies. Forever outrageous, Jayne is still rock'n'roll's answer to Lenny Bruce and continues to record and perform. Jayne's marvellous memoirs *Man Enough To Be A Woman* were published by Serpent's Tail in 1995.

Frenchy. The valet to the Dolls lost his apartment and the New York Dolls in one fell swoop. After telling his friends he was going to visit his family, he was never heard from again.

Elda Gentile. Currently working as a producer of radio programmes for Woodstock Communications, Elda still sings and writes articles for *New York Waste* magazine. She is planning a television show called *Rock Trash*, with Debbie Harry as the host.

Bob Gruen. Among the best known rock photographers in the world, his pictures can be seen in *Chaos! The Sex Pistols* (Omnibus) and *Sometime In New York City* (Genesis) amongst numerous other books and publications.

David Johansen (a.k.a. Buster Poindexter). Married to photographer Kate Simon, Johansen maintains a successful career as Buster Poindexter. He scored an international hit with 'Hot, Hot, Hot' in 1987. With several films to his credit, including *Scrooged* with Bill Murray and *Car 54, Where Are You?*, he makes the time to sift through scripts but doesn't actively pursue roles. "I do little bits here and there. I don't go chasing after it. If somebody comes after me and wants me to do something, I consider it."

Peter Jordan. "I'm in my mid-20s! I have three children, my daughter is 22, a little older than me and I have a daughter who is 10 and a son of eight. After leaving the Dolls, I played with Robert Gordon, Link Wray and Jayne County. I had Stumblebunny, then The Nightcaps. I've done music for commercials and session work. I retired from music in 1988 and I'm now a concierge."

Arthur Kane. Arthur has lived in LA for a number of years. He has toyed with the idea of putting together an all-star travelling version of The New York Dolls, with the likes of former Hanoi Rocks vocalist Mike Monroe and Gilbey Clarke of Guns N' Roses but is aware of the difficulties of pulling off such a project. "How far would it go? I'm not a teenager anymore. Are we going to put all the make-up on and stuff?" Kane is still in regular contact with Rick Rivets, with whom he may start another band in the future.

Eliott Kidd. "Like most of the people from our crowd, I'm trying to put my health back together. It's amazing that I lived.

I'm sick of the music business, it's a good business for every-body but the musicians. I moved to LA, I needed a change of scenery. Someone convinced me that there's lots of parts for New York guys in mob movies and someone just gave me a script. I know the percentages of having a career in acting are slim so I'm not going to get crazy about it." Sadly, Elliott died in 1998.

Steve Leber. Although no longer in business with David Krebs, Steve Leber is still heavily involved in the entertainment industry. "In the Eighties we decided to reduce the amount of management that we did and mind our catalogues. We had the AC/DC catalogue, the Aerosmith catalogue and several others – meaning the records, the masters and the publishing, and concentrated on those. We also started to produce shows when music was going through a rap and country phase. It's only been in the last couple of years that there is room again for rock'n'roll, so we're going back into bands again. We don't believe in stealing big name bands, we build from the ground up, building the new Aerosmiths, the new Dolls. We're managing four new bands and starting all over again."

Malcolm McLaren. Following the dissolution of The Sex Pistols, McLaren managed Bow Wow Wow. In the early Eighties, he began a solo recording career with the album, *Duck Rock*, which is presently being remixed by both old school and modern hip hop producers. He pillaged Puccini for *Fans* in 1984 and attempted to recreate the romance of Paris with an LP of the same title in 1994. He is currently managing Jungk, a band from the Far East, who have just made their New York début. He remembers the Dolls with fondness. "Girl's under-wear never looked the same again."

Paul Nelson. Still a resident of New York, Nelson is now a video historian. Although he backed off from the music business, he is involved in archival research and writes the occasional article.

Rick Rivets (a.k.a. George Fedorcik). "I'm not working on anything right now although Arthur wants to start a band up with me and his ex-wife, Babs. She looks good but I don't know how she sings. I've also been playing with some people out in the Hamptons, jamming . . . we might put something together."

Sabel Starr (a.k.a. Sabel Shields). "It was so hard to talk about things. My life has been so normal for the last 20 years." Sabel lives in Nevada with her two children, Christian, who is 12 and Donnay, 18. She works at Herrod's Casino as a 21 dealer. She told the author: "It's funny because I was so much a part of the scene. Debbie Harry and I stayed in touch for years. I have no regrets, Iggy sums it up in that song he wrote 'Look Away'. It may sound horrifying, I'd been with him also, when I was 13, but it wasn't back then, it was all fun. Although, when I left the scene, I left it for good." Corel Shields is now a housewife, leading a similarly quiet life to that of her sister. 'Look Away', Pop's poignant ballad of Johnny, Sabel and the Ig can be found on his *Naughty Little Doggie* album (Virgin) which contains the lyric: 'Unfortunately the needle broke/Their rock and roll love like a bicycle spoke/I found her in a back street/With her looks half gone/She was selling something/That I was on/Look away . . .'"

Gail Higgins Smith. After the Dolls split up, Gail worked as The Heartbreaker's tour manager. She has lived in London for many years and has turned an abiding interest in Fifties clothing, decor and lifestyle into a creative business. Between running two shops, she finds the time to host her own club nights under the pseudonym of Sparkle Moore.

Sylvain Sylvain (a.k.a. Sylvain Mizrahi). Sylvain settled in Los Angeles, where he had a band but . . . "I had to get my son out of there, it was like a zoo and there was nothing happening. I had a great band there but nobody was paying any attention. I was playing live, making a lot of people happy as I've always done through the years but no deal, no offer, nothing." Sylvain and O'dell relocated to Georgia, the hometown of his long time partner, Wanda. He recently signed to the Cleveland based label, Fishhead, and has recorded a new album for them called *Sleep Baby Doll*. He is planning to tour in the States. When asked for the name of his new outfit, Sylvain commented: "I've had too many new names, y'know." Sylvain went from The Criminals, then had The Teardrops, then The 14th Street Band, then Teenage News. "I'm a New York Doll. I told that to my record company, I said please, put it on the top of the release – The New York Dolls' Sylvain Sylvain. Whatever I do, it's going to be compared to the Dolls. No matter who I play with or what happens. Why hide it, baby, c'mon out the front with it!"

Marty Thau. Almost immediately after he left Steve Leber in charge of the Dolls, Thau was financially rewarded from an earlier investment in a song that became a smash 'Life Is A Rock (But The Radio Rolled Me)' which was recorded by session musicians under the name of Reunion. It was his last link with the mainstream music business. He found a new niche in the NY punk scene and formed his own Red Star label, which was responsible for releases by Suicide and Richard Hell and The Voidoids, amongst others. After Red Star's fortune dimmed, Thau became a partner in an executive recruiting firm. He has just reactivated Red Star and is planning to release a CD of the Dolls live in Paris, '74.

Cyrinda Foxe-Tyler. "I've raised a child (Mia, half sister to actress Liv Tyler). I'm back in New York, I'm single. I've written a book (*Dream On* published by Dove). It's about my life but it also has a lot in it about Steven Tyler. I did a lot of promotion for it, television and radio. So much so that radio is now my favourite medium so I'd like to have my own radio show. I could be a rock and roll mom with kids calling in to tell me their problems and also I'd play music." Sadly, Cyrinda, who in the opinion of Sylvain was an honorary female Doll, died in 2002.

Sleep Baby Doll

Sleep baby doll
Don't you cry now
All said and done
Play guitar/You did fine now
'Cos I love what you do
My sweet baby doll

Johnny Boy
Little altar boy
As they all say
You always had a slice of God in you
From Billy's mom's basement
To God
What more can you say

Sleep baby doll
Don't you cry now
After said and done
You did fine now
'Cos they loved what you do
My sweet baby doll
Oh baby
My sweet baby doll

Oh Billy Doll
You were one of the first
As you were struggling to keep up those back bones
I know that really must have hurt
You were the personality
And the crisis

Sleep baby dolls
Don't you cry now
After said and done
Sleep awhile now
'Cos they loved what you left
Left us a lot of your heart
Oh baby
My sweet baby doll

Jerry – you're the little heart of Gene Krupa
You were never the replacement
Always the originator
Drive that motorcycle

Sleep baby doll
Don't you cry now
After said and done
Sleep good night now
'Cos I love what you do
My sweet baby doll
Oh babies
My sweet baby doll

Lyrics to 'Sleep Baby Doll' by Sylvain Sylvain (1997).
Permission to reproduce from Fishhead Records.

The New York Dolls' Discography

SINGLES

JETBOY/VIETNAMESE BABY
(UK, 7″) 1973 Mercury 6 052 402

JETBOY/VIETNAMESE BABY
(PORTUGAL, 7″) 1973 Mercury 6 052 402

TRASH (MONO)/TRASH (STEREO)
(US, 7″) 1973 Mercury DJ-378 (73414) (promo only)

PERSONALITY CRISIS/PERSONALITY CRISIS
(US, 7″) 1973 Mercury DJ-387 (promo only)

TRASH/PERSONALITY CRISIS
(SPAIN, 7″) 1973 Mercury 6 052 372

PERSONALITY CRISIS/TRASH
(US, 7″) 1973 Mercury 73414

PERSONALITY CRISIS/TRASH
(SWEDEN, 7″) 1973 Mercury 6052732

STRANDED IN THE JUNGLE/DON'T START ME TALKING
(SPAIN, 7″) 1973 Mercury 6-52 655

JETBOY/VIETNAMESE BABY
(NETHER., 7″) 1973 Mercury 6 052 402

STRANDED IN THE JUNGLE/WHO ARE THE MYSTERY GIRLS
(US, 7″) 1974 Mercury 73478

STRANDED IN THE JUNGLE/WHO ARE THE MYSTERY GIRLS
(US, 7″) 1974 Mercury 73478

WHO ARE THE MYSTERY GIRLS/STRANDED IN THE JUNGLE
(UK, 7″) 1974 Mercury 6 052 615

STRANDED IN THE JUNGLE/WHO ARE THE MYSTERY GIRLS
(GERMANY, 7″) 1974 Mercury 6 052 615

STRANDED IN THE JUNGLE/WHO ARE THE MYSTERY GIRLS
(JAPAN, 7″) 1974 Mercury SFL-1855

BABYLON/HUMAN BEING
(FRANCE, 7″) 1974, Mercury 6 837 207

JETBOY/BABYLON/WHO ARE THE MYSTERY GIRLS
(UK, 7″) 1977 Mercury 6 160 008

BAD GIRL/SUBWAY TRAIN
(GERMANY, 7″) 1978 Bellaphon BF 18608

PERSONALITY CRISIS/LOOKING FOR A KISS
(GERMANY, 7″) 1978 Bellaphon BF 18576

PILLS/DOWN, DOWN, DOWNTOWN
(FRANCE, 7″) 1984 Fan Club NYD 1

PERSONALITY CRISIS/SUBWAY TRAIN
(NETHER., 7″) 1986 Antler DOLLS 1

LOOKING FOR A KISS/BAD GIRL
(NETHER., 7″) 1986 Antler DOLLS 2

PERSONALITY CRISIS/LOOKING FOR A KISS/
SUBWAY TRAIN/BAD GIRL
(UK, 12″) 1982 Kamera ERA 013

PERSONALITY CRISIS/SUBWAY TRAIN
(NETHER., 12″) 1986 Antler DOLLS 1

LOOKING FOR A KISS/BAD GIRL
(NETHER., 12″) 1986 Antler DOLLS 2

PERSONALITY CRISIS
(UK, 12″) 1990 See For Miles SEA 3

THE EARLY YEARS LIVE
(UK, 12″) 1990 Receiver REPLAY 3011

ALBUMS

NEW YORK DOLLS
(US, LP) 1973 Mercury SRM-1-675

NEW YORK DOLLS
(UK, LP) 1973 Mercury 6 338 270

NEW YORK DOLLS
(FRANCE, LP) 1973 Mercury 6 398 004

NEW YORK DOLLS
(SPAIN, LP) 1973 Mercury 6338270

NEW YORK DOLLS
(NETHER., LP) 1973 Mercury 6 336 280

NEW YORK DOLLS
(JAPAN, LP) 1973 Mercury RJ-5 103

TOO MUCH TOO SOON
(US, LP) 1974 Mercury SRM-1-1001

TOO MUCH TOO SOON
(UK, LP) 1974 Mercury 6 338 498

TOO MUCH TOO SOON
(FRANCE, LP) 1974 Mercury 9 100 002

TOO MUCH TOO SOON
(SPAIN, LP) 1974 Mercury 63 38 498

TOO MUCH TOO SOON
(NETHER., LP) 1974 Mercury 6 463 064

TOO MUCH TOO SOON
(AUSTRALIA, LP) 1974 Mercury 6338 498 1

TOO MUCH TOO SOON
(JAPAN, LP) 1974 Mercury RJ-5135

THE VERY BEST OF THE NEW YORK DOLLS
(JAPAN, LP) 1977 Mercury RJ-7234

NEW YORK DOLLS/TOO MUCH TOO SOON
(UK, LP) 1977 Mercury 6641631

RED PATENT LEATHER
(FRANCE, LP) 1984 Fan Club FC 007

NIGHT OF THE LIVING DOLLS
(US, LP) 1985 Mercury 826094-1 M-1

NIGHT OF THE LIVING DOLLS
(JAPAN, LP) 1985 25 PP-186

ROCK LEGENDS a.k.a. TOO MUCH TOO SOON
(AUSTRALIA, LP) 1986 Mercury 6 463 029

NEW YORK DOLLS/TOO MUCH TOO SOON
(UK, LP) 1986 Mercury PRID 12

LIPSTICK KILLERS
(FRANCE, LP) 1990 Danceteria DANLP 038

NEW YORK DOLLS
(US, CD) 1987 Mercury 832 752-2

TOO MUCH TOO SOON
(US, CD) 1987 Mercury 834 230-2

NEW YORK DOLLS + TOO MUCH TOO SOON
(JAPAN, CD) 1987 Mercury 33PD-422

RED PATENT LEATHER
(FRANCE, CD) 1988 Fan Club FC 007

CLASSIC TRACKS
(UK, CD) 1988 Counterpoint CDEP14

NEW YORK DOLLS
(JAPAN, CD) 1989 Mercury 23PD110

TOO MUCH TOO SOON
(JAPAN, CD) 1989 Mercury 23PD111

LIPSTICK KILLERS
(FRANCE, CD) 1990 Danceteria DANCD 038

LIPSTICK KILLERS
(US, CD) 1990 Roir 88561-5027-2

SUPER BEST COLLECTION
(JAPAN, CD) 1990 Teichiku TECP-28513

RED PATENT LEATHER
(JAPAN, CD) 1990 Teichiku TECP-25234

NEW YORK DOLLS
(JAPAN, CD) 1991 Mercury PHCR-6043

TOO MUCH TOO SOON
(JAPAN, CD) 1991 Mercury PHCR-6044

SEVEN DAY WEEKEND
(UK, CD) 1992 Receiver RRCD 163

LIVE IN NYC 1975
(US, CD) 1992 Restless 7 72596-2

NEW YORK TAPES '72–'73
(FRANCE, CD) 1993 Skydog 62257-2

PARIS BURNING
(FRANCE, CD) 1993 Skydog 62256-2

EVIL DOLLS – NEW YORK TAPES '72–'73
(JAPAN, CD) 1993 Meldac MECR-25025

PARIS IS BURNING
(JAPAN, CD) 1993 Mercury MECR-25023

PARIS LE TRASH
(US, CD) 1993 Tripe X 51116-2

ROCK'N'ROLL
(US, CD) 1994 Mercury 314 522 129-2

ROCK'N'ROLL
(GERMANY, CD) 1994 Mercury 522 129-2

ROCK'N'ROLL
(JAPAN, CD) 1994 Mercury PHCH-1327

TOO MUCH TOO SOON
(JAPAN, CD) 1994 Mercury PHCR-4241

LIPSTICK KILLERS
(FRANCE, CD) 1996 Danceteria RE 104CD

PARIS IS BURNING
(JAPAN, CD) 1996 Teichiku TECW-20369

EVIL DOLLS – NEW YORK TAPES '72–'73
(JAPAN, CD) 1996 Teichiku TECW-20370

NEW YORK DOLLS
(US, K7) 1973 Mercury MCR-4-1-675

TOO MUCH TOO SOON
(US, K7) 1974 Mercury MCR-4-1-1001

LIPSTICK KILLERS
(US, K7) 1981 Roir A-104

RED PATENT LEATHER
(FRANCE, K7) 1984 Fan Club FCK 007

NIGHT OF THE LIVING DOLLS
(US, K7) 1985 Mercury 826094-4 M-1

NEW YORK DOLLS/TOO MUCH TOO SOON
(UK, K7) 1986 Mercury PRIDC 12

NEW YORK DOLLS
(US, 8 TAPES) 1973 Mercury MC-8-1-675

TOO MUCH TOO SOON
(US, 8 TAPES) 1974 Mercury MC-8-1-1001

BOOTLEGS

LOOKING FOR A KISS/WHO ARE THE MYSTERY GIRLS –
SOMETHIN' ELSE
(US, 7″) 1974 Trash TR-001

LOOKING FOR A KISS/WHO ARE THE MYSTERY GIRLS –
SOMETHIN' ELSE
(US, 7″) 1982 Trash TR-001

REHEARSAL & LIVE EP
(US, 7″) 1989 NYD NYD 101

REHEARSAL & LIVE EP
(US, 7″) 1989 NYD NYD 101

LONELY PLANET BOY/BABYLON (the rough mixes)
(FRANCE, 7″) 1998 Sucksex SEX 15

DOLL HOUSE LIVE IN L.A.
(US, 10″) 1988 Lipstick Killer JUNK 74

DALLAS '74
(US, LP) 1977 Smilin' Ears 7707

LIVE IN PARIS 23/12/73
(FRANCE, LP) 1984 Thunders 6381007

TRASH (don't take my life away)
(FRANCE, LP) 1984 Desdemona DES-2013

DIZZY DOLLS
(ITALY, LP) 1988 (Unknown) 72/74

LOOKING FOR A KISS
(FRANCE, LP) 1989 Company GF 46

7 DAY WEEKEND
(US, LP) 1991 Brigand LIP 73

BACK IN THE USA
(FRANCE, CD) 1991 Speedball SBC 015

7 DAY WEEKEND
(GERMANY, CD) 1991 Chapter One CO 25159

ENDLESS PARTY
(ITALY, CD) 1991 Triangle PYCD 067

EUROPE 1973
(ITALY, CD) 1992 The Welfare Pig TWP-CD-208

VIVE LA FRANCE
(ITALY, CD) 1992 (Unknown) 92–DLL-SC-4007

LIVE USA
(GERMANY, CD) 1993 PR-Record imm 40.90155

DAWN OF THE DOLLS (Actress Session)
(US CD) 1977 FAB Discs CD 0001